D1520756

FOREWORD

As the only living Commanding Officer of an Iowa class battleship, or any other class of battleship, I was encouraged to write the Foreword for a book on the battleship USS Missouri and offer my reflections on having had the privilege of commanding such an impressive and legendary naval ship.

Being born and raised in the land-locked State of Arkansas, I had never imagined myself making a career in the U. S. Navy. Born in Fort Smith and moving to Hot Springs with my family between the fourth and fifth grade, I slowly began to imagine myself as an attorney when I graduated from college and didn't give much thought to a career in the military.

However, when I graduated from Hendrix College in Conway, Arkansas, in 1961, I faced the near certainty of being drafted into the Army and, after considerable thought, and having heard a lot of "sea stories" from my "Uncle Bill," I decided that the Navy would be a better choice. As a result, I responded to a group of Navy recruiters who came on campus during my final semester and signed up for Officer Candidate School (OCS) as my next chapter in life.

I graduated OCS and was ordered to the USS Princeton (LPH 5) (a converted WW II aircraft carrier converted to an Amphibious Assault ship) as my first tour of duty. I flew out to the Philippines, went aboard, and was assigned as the Assistant Personnel Officer. Following 5 days in port in Subic Bay, we got underway because a typhoon was boiling up through the South China Sea and we had to get underway that very day. It was my first time underway at sea and we went out into 40 to 60-foot waves. Surprisingly enough, I never got sea sick or even got queasy during that, or any other time in heavy seas.

Six months later I was advanced to Assistant Navigator which I performed for two-and-a-half years. I did most all of the celestial and terrestrial navigation while working for 3 different commanders, all aviators. I also qualified as an Officer of the Deck (OOD) while still an Ensign.

One of the most interesting events of my early career was, as OOD one afternoon, we had mail call and the Boatswain's Mate of the watch handed me a letter through the bridge porthole. It turned out to be from the Hot Springs Draft Board and indicated I had been drafted into the Army. Well, that was a real shocker because, at that relatively young age, I wasn't sure if they could actually do that or not. After some thought, I tore it up and threw it in the trash can, but worried for weeks about my future.

Near the end of my tour aboard the Princeton, I received a letter from the Navy offering me a transition from the Navy Reserve to the Regular Navy and, after considerable thought, I decided to make a full career out of the Navy. After a tour of duty at the Navy's "Destroyer School" I spent a good part of my career aboard a string of destroyers, culminating in the commissioning of, and commanding, a brand-new Spruance Class destroyer, a gas turbine powered 7½ ton destroyer, the USS Leftwich.

Other assignments followed, both on shore and at sea, including duty at the Pentagon as the Program Director of the Aegis Shipbuilding and Weapons Development Program, however the jewel in the crown was when I was given Command of the Battleship Missouri (BB-63).

I consider it a high honor to have been among the twenty men selected for, and entrusted with, the command of one of the finest warships in the United States Navy and for the opportunity to serve with the sailors that sailed aboard her.

Al Carney

Hot Springs, Arkansas

March 2021

U.S.S. MISSOURI

THE "MIGHTY MO" AND THE MEN WHO SAILED HER

By
Scott Baron

Copyright © by Scott Baron, 2021

ISBN: 9798735729518

All Rights Reserved

Table of Contents

Introduction

On March 31, 1992, as Captain Albert Lee Kaiss stepped off the quarterdeck of the battleship USS *Missouri* (BB-63), turned to salute the ensign, then proceeded down the gangway, he was making naval history. He was the last man off the last battleship, making him in essence the last battleship sailor.

He was also the only Commanding Officer in the history of the US Navy to both put a Navy ship into commission, and take the same ship out of commission, having commanded her twice. Nor was she an ordinary warship. The USS *Missouri* was a legend.

One of only four Iowa-class battleships, she was born at the start of the Second World War, and although she would get into the fight late, she would still see action as part of the first naval air strike on the Japanese home islands, bombard the shores of Iwo Jima and Okinawa before anchoring in Tokyo Bay to receive the Japanese surrender.

Missouri would see her second war in Korea, fighting first North Koreans and later Chinese Communists off the shores of North Korea. Placed into the reserve fleet following the Korean War, she became a tourist attraction for the next 29 years before being called to serve in the Iraq War, her third conflict. After again being decommissioned, she sailed one last time to Pearl Harbor where she currently resides as a museum ship, within sight of the USS Arizona Memorial, in a sense the Alpha-Omega of America's War against Japan.

Launch and Commissioning

The keel for the USS *Missouri* was laid down at the Brooklyn Navy Yard on January 6, 1941, under the direction of Rear Admiral Clark H. Woodward. Although the United States was not yet at war, preparations were being made for her eventual entry. *Missouri* would be the fourth of four Iowa-class battleships.

The ship was launched on January 29, 1944 and before a crowd of 20,000 to 30,000 spectators, Margaret Truman, the daughter of Harry S. Truman, christened the ship. Truman, one of the senators from the ship's namesake state of Missouri, gave a speech at the ceremony. The work of fitting-out the ship proceeded quickly, and the ship was commissioned on June 11, 1944 with Captain William Callaghan her first commanding officer.

Missouri was 887 feet in length with a beam of 108 feet and a draft of 36 feet. She was powered by 8 × Babcock & Wilcox boilers which created 212,000 shaft horsepower propelling 4 steam turbines and 4 screw propellers.

Missouri could steam at a top speed of 32.5 knots (37.4 mph) and a range of 15,000 miles at 15 knots. Her crew consisted of 117 officers and 1,804 enlisted men.

As a modern warship, she was armed with a formidable array of weapons, including nine 16-inch/50 caliber Mark 7 guns in three triple gun armored turrets, two forward and one aft. The secondary battery consisted of twenty 5-inch/38 caliber dual purpose guns mounted in twin turrets clustered amidships, five turrets on either side. Anti-aircraft armament consisted of eighty 40 mm Bofors guns and forty-nine 20 mm auto-cannon in twin and single mounts. She would demonstrate her proficiency with weapons in three wars.

U.S.S. MISSOURI

Captain William M. Callaghan

Missouri's first captain, William Callaghan would command her for the majority of her service during WW II. William McCombe Callaghan was born in Oakland, California on August 8, 1897, the second son born to businessman Charles William Callaghan and his wife, Rose Wheeler Callaghan and he and his older brother Daniel were raised as devout Roman Catholics.

Daniel Callaghan, seven years William's senior, would later become a US Navy rear admiral and be awarded a posthumous Medal of Honor. Both brothers studied at Saint Ignatius College Preparatory in San Francisco, Daniel graduating in the class of 1907 and William seven years later in 1914.

Callaghan attended the University of California and Drew's Preparatory School before being appointed to the US Naval Academy from the state of California on June 11,1915. His brother Daniel also attended Annapolis, graduating with the class of 1911.

His class was ordered to active service with the entrance of the United States into World War I and Callaghan graduated early and was commissioned an ensign in the US Navy on June 7, 1918. He was assigned to the battleship USS *Wisconsin* (BB-9) under the command of Captain David Foote Sellers. Stationed aboard her from June through August 1918, *Wisconsin* was assigned to the Coast Battleship Patrol Squadron, but was used primarily as a training ship.

U.S.S. MISSOURI

In August 1918, Callaghan was assigned aboard the newly commissioned USS *Stevens* (DD-86) a Wickes-class destroyer operating out of Queenstown, Ireland. Assigned to the United States Naval Forces, Europe, *Stevens* operated out of that port and protected convoys on the Queenstown-Liverpool circuit until mid-December.

With the armistice in November 11, *Wisconsin* sailed for home on December 16, 1918 and, after stops at the Azores and Bermuda, entered Boston in January 1919, but Callaghan, promoted to the temporary rank of Lt.(jg), was not aboard, having been assigned to the Sampson-class destroyer USS *Allen* (DD-66) in December.

With the war over, *Allen* helped to escort the USS *George Washington*, with President Woodrow Wilson embarked, into Brest, France, on December 13th. Following that mission, the destroyer returned to Queenstown, whence she departed on the day after Christmas, bound for home arriving in New York on January 7, 1919.

The *Allen* patrolled the East Coast and West Indies as part of the United States Atlantic Fleet. That duty continued until June 22, 1922, when she was placed out of commission, in reserve. (She would be placed back into commission three years later, on June 23, 1925.

Callaghan transferred to the USS *Champlin* (DD-104), a Wickes-class destroyer, on July 28, 1919 but only remained one month, taking her from New York to San Diego before reporting aboard the destroyer USS *Hamilton* (DD-141) in August as the Engineer Officer.

Based at San Diego, *Hamilton* participated in battle practice and maneuvers along the California coast with Destroyer Squadron 17. In mid-1920 she also took part in torpedo and smoke screen operations in Hawaii.

While aboard *Hamilton*, Callaghan was promoted to the permanent rank of Lieutenant (jg), on July 1, 1920. In October, Callaghan was assigned as Engineer Officer aboard the USS *Nicholas* (DD-311)

The *Nicholas* was a Clemson-class destroyer commissioned at the Mare Island Naval Yard on November 23, 1920, the first Navy ship named for Samuel Nicholas, the first Commandant of the United States Marine Corps. She operated off San Diego until being wrecked in the Honda Point Disaster, September 8, 1923.

6

On January 4, 1921, Callaghan shipped over to the Clemson-class destroyer USS *Dent* (DD-116). The Dent was recommissioned on December 14, 1920, although with a reduced complement of men. She took part in gunnery and torpedo practice and in fleet maneuvers. She also paid port calls at South America and Mexico in January through March 1921, before she was decommissioned for the second time on June 7, 1922.

June through August 1921, Callaghan was assigned to the USS Farquhar (DD-304) a WW I era Clemson-class destroyer, transferring in August to the USS *Twiggs* (DD-127) a Wickes-class destroyer as Engineer where he remained until November 1921 when he was assigned aboard the USS *Sloat* (DD 316).

The *Sloat*, a Clemson-class destroyer commissioned on December 30, 1920 with Lieutenant Commander J R. Palmer in command, was placed in reserve shortly after arriving in San Diego on January 24, 1921.

She came out of reserve in October and conducted gunnery exercises during the winter and carried out torpedo trials in April and May 1922. On June 3, 1922, Callaghan was promoted to full lieutenant and 5 days later, she sailed with the fleet for Puget Sound and operated in that area until returning to San Diego on September 19.

On February 6, 1923, she departed San Diego with the fleet, and conducted exercises off Panama until returning on April 11, spending most of the remainder of the year, and much of the next, undergoing repairs at Mare Island.

Callaghan reported to the Naval Postgraduate School at Annapolis in the summer of 1923 for postgraduate instruction in electrical engineering and he completed the course at Columbia University, New York City, receiving the degree of Master of Science in September 1925, after which he was assigned to sea duty aboard the USS *Concord* (CL-10), an Omaha-class light cruiser, originally classified as a scout cruiser. She was the fourth Navy ship named for the town of Concord, Massachusetts, the site of the first battle of the American Revolution. She spent the first nine years of her career in the Atlantic assigned as part of the Scouting Force.

U.S.S. MISSOURI

In October 1928, Callaghan was detailed to Washington DC at the Navy's Bureau of Engineering assigned to the Repairs Division until May 1930 when he reported to the Lexington-class carrier USS *Saratoga* (CV-3) as the assistant engineering officer.

The *Saratoga* participated in fleet exercises off the coast of Panama and became a sort of movie star when the 1932 movie *Hell Divers* was filmed aboard the ship. The film starred Wallace Beery and a young Clark Gable as a pair of competing aircraft gunners assigned to VF-1B. Scenes from the 1933 Joe E. Brown film comedy, *Son of a Sailor*, were also filmed aboard *Saratoga* and featured the flight deck of the ship and members of her crew.

Callaghan was promoted to Lieutenant Commander on July 1, 1932, and he returned to the Naval Academy in May 1933 teaching Marine Engineering.

On June 15, 1936, Lt. Commander Callaghan relieved Lt. Commander Nicholas Vytlacil as captain of the USS *Reuben James* (DD-245), a post-World War One, four-funnel Clemson-class destroyer and his first command.

USS Reuben James (DD-245)

The *James* operated in the Pacific, homeported out of San Diego, California. Relieved by Lt. Commander Edward C. Metcalfe on May 10, 1938.

(The *Reuben James* was later sunk by a torpedo attack from German submarine U-552 near Iceland on October 31, 1941, before the U.S. had officially joined the war.)

Callaghan was promoted to commander on June 23, 1938 and that May, he reported as executive officer aboard the USS *Henderson* (AP-1) a transport, commissioned in 1917. The ship was primarily engaged in carrying replacements for the fleet and the Marines in China.

In May 1939, Callaghan was back in Washington DC, assigned to the Office of Chief of Naval Operations, coordinating ship movements. In August 1941, with war on the horizon, Callaghan was sent to England for a month as a Naval Observer at the American Embassy in London, returning to Washington in September 1941 where he remained until July 10, 1942.

That July, Callaghan was transferred to the Staff of Admiral Chester W. Nimitz the Commander in Chief, US Pacific Fleet (COMPAFLT) with his headquarters at Pearl Harbor, Hawaii, with a promotion to captain on September 8, 1942.

Callaghan was awarded the Legion of Merit for his service as an Assistant War Plans Officer. His citation states:

"For exceptionally meritorious conduct…as Assistant War Plans Officer for Logistics and Assistant Logistics Officer, Pacific Fleet, during operations against enemy Japanese forces in the Pacific War Area from July 10, 1942 to May 1, 1944. During this period, Rear Admiral (then Captain) Callaghan skillfully assisted in the planning for logistical support of the Navy and shore-based establishment engaged in the campaigns for the capture of the Gilbert and Marshall Islands and their subsequent maintenance. Assisting in organizing the Logistics Division of the Joint Staff of Commander in Chief, Pacific Fleet and Pacific Ocean Areas, he was instrumental in developing its operational methods and procedure…"

On June 11, 1944, Callaghan took command of the newly commissioned USS *Missouri*. the last battleship commissioned by the US Navy. She conducted her initial sea trials off New York, beginning on July 10, and then proceeded south to Chesapeake Bay, where she embarked on a shakedown cruise and conducted combat training.

During this period, she operated with the cruiser USS *Alaska*, (CB-1) which had also recently entered service, and several escorting destroyers. The ship got underway on November 11, bound for the West Coast of the United States. She passed through the Panama Canal on November 18 and continued on to San Francisco. There, additional fitting-out work was carried out to prepare the vessel for use as a fleet flagship.

U.S.S. MISSOURI

Missouri departed San Francisco on December 14, enroute to Ulithi in the Caroline Islands, where she joined the rest of the fleet on January 13, 1945. She became a temporary headquarters ship for Vice Admiral Marc A. Mitscher.

She then joined the Fast Carrier Task Force, Task Force 58, which sortied on 27 January. Missouri served as part of the anti-aircraft screen and tasked with defending the aircraft carrier *Lexington*. By February 16, the task force had arrived off the coast of Japan to begin a series of air strikes.

On December 14, *Missouri* departed San Francisco and sailed for Ulithi in the Caroline Islands, where she joined the rest of the fleet on January 13, 1945. She became a temporary headquarters ship for Vice Admiral Marc A. Mitscher. She then joined the Fast Carrier Task Force, Task Force 58, (TF-58) which sortied on January 27.

The *Missouri* joined Task Group 58.2 (TG 58.2) comprised of the carriers USS *Lexington* (CV-16), USS *Hancock* (CV-19), USS *San Jacinto* (CVL-30), the battleship USS *Wisconsin* (BB-64), the cruisers USS *San Francisco* (CA-38) and USS *Boston* (CA-69), and 19 destroyers.

As part of the plan to deceive the Japanese and cover the landings at Iwo Jima, the U.S. Fast Carrier Task Force (TF 58) conducted the first carrier strikes on the Japanese home islands on February 16-17, 1945, the first air strikes against Japan since the famed Doolittle raid that had launched from carrier USS *Hornet* (CV-8) on April 18, 1942.

TF-58 next sailed to support the landings at Iwo Jima and joined the bombardment force at Iwo Jima D-day, February 19, 1945 and although aircraft from TF 58 would conduct strikes on Iwo Jima, the great majority of air support to pre-landing strikes and subsequent support of Marines ashore was carried out by the ten escort carriers of Task Group 52.2 (Support Carrier Group), commanded by Rear Admiral Calvin T. Durgin. On February 19, *Missouri* shot down a Japanese plane, her first aircraft kill of the war.

Missouri provided gunfire support to the marines until Task Force 58 departed for Ulithi on March 5 in order to replenish fuel and ammunition where *Missouri* was transferred to the Yorktown task group.

The ships departed again on March 14 to stage another round of airstrikes on Japan. Four days later, *Missouri*'s anti-aircraft guns assisted in the destruction of four Japanese aircraft while carrier aircraft struck a variety of targets around the Inland Sea, which prompted a Japanese counter-attack that struck several carriers.

During the battle, the carrier USS *Franklin* was badly-damaged and *Missouri*'s task group was detached to cover her withdrawal. By March 22, *Franklin* had left the area of operations and *Missouri's* group returned to the fleet to join in the preparatory bombardment for the upcoming invasion of Okinawa.

On March 24, Missouri took part in the bombardment of the southern coast of Okinawa as part of an effort to distract Japanese attention away from the actual invasion target on the western side of the island. On April 1, American ground forces landed.

While operating with the carriers on April 11, *Missouri* came under attack from a Japanese A6M *Zero*, a Kamikaze, or low-flying suicide plane which penetrated the curtain of her shells to crash just below her main deck level and the impact shattered the aircraft and the starboard wing of the plane detached, throwing gasoline on the deck that rapidly ignited, starting a gasoline fire at 5-inch Gun Mount No. 3.

The plane's 500-pound bomb did not detonate. The *Missouri* suffered only superficial damage, the fire was quickly suppressed, and the ship remained on station. Parts of the plane's wreckage and the top half of the pilot's body landed on board Missouri and the plane's wing was turned over to the crew to be cut up for souvenirs.

Despite protests from the crew, who wanted to hose the remains over the deck, Callaghan insisted that the young Japanese airman had done his duty with honor and deserved a military funeral. A corpsman, Stephen Cromwell, later recalled:

"I was able to recover his body and I called up to the bridge to ask if I should throw it overboard ... Captain Callaghan said, 'No, when we secure, take it down to the sick bay, and we'll have a burial for him tomorrow." Following examination, the remains were placed in a canvas bag with dummy shell casings to weigh it down.

The following day, the Japanese pilot received a military funeral at sea. A Japanese flag, improvised by one of the ship's bosun's mates, covered the bag holding the man's remains. The ship's chaplain gave a brief prayer and committed the body to the sea and the six pallbearers let it slide overboard, accompanied by a volley of rifle fire.

Callaghan's decision on the Japanese pilot's funeral in 1945 earned praise years later, although a memorial service aboard the *Missouri* in April 2001 attracted some controversy. Leading up to the service, Callaghan's son said, "*My father believed a burial at sea for the pilot was the right thing to do. He felt it would set a good example for the crew in showing respect for the life of people, even for the people you are opposing.*"

Junko Kamata, a niece of one of the Japanese pilots killed in the April 1945 battle, said, "*I want to thank Captain Callaghan for his humanitarian consideration for kamikaze soldiers.*" Minoru Shibuya, Japanese Consul General, called Callaghan's actions "*a glorious deed, to salute the [pilot's] bravery.*"

Daniel Inouye, US Senator from Hawaii, reflected that "from the dawn of civilization, warriors respected their adversaries; it was an unspoken code of honor. When Callaghan saw the broken body of his sworn enemy lying upon his ship, he saw him not as an enemy, but simply as a man." (The identity of the Japanese pilot has been narrowed to three possibilities: Lieutenant Junior Grade Shigeju Yaguchi, Petty Officer Second Class Takashi Sogabe, and Petty Officer Second Class Setsuo Ishino. An information plaque on board USS Missouri in December 2011 advocates the view that the pilot was most likely Ishino.)

Six days later, *Missouri* detected a Japanese submarine about 14 miles from the task group. The light aircraft carrier USS *Bataan* (CVL-29) and four destroyers were detached, resulting in the sinking of the submarine I-56.

Missouri left Task Force 58 on May 5 to return to Ulithi. In the course of her operations off Okinawa, she claimed five aircraft shot down and another probable kill, along with partial credit for another six aircraft destroyed.

Captain William M. Callaghan

On May 9, *Missouri* reached Ulithi, and on May 14, Callaghan turned command of *Missouri* to Captain Stuart S. Murray, a classmate of his from the US Naval Academy. On May 18, Admiral William F. Halsey Jr., the commander of Third Fleet, came aboard the ship making her the fleet flagship.

Callaghan was briefly assigned to the staff of Commander US Pacific Fleet until July 1945 when he was called back to Washington DC to serve in the Office of Chief of Naval Operations as the Assistant. Chief of Naval Operations for Transportation.

On May 24, 1945, Callaghan was promoted to Rear Admiral, to rank from August 11, 1943. In August 1948, Callaghan was named Commander Training Command Atlantic Fleet where he remained until November 30, 1949 when he became the first to command the Military Sea Transportation Service. He was promoted to the 3-star rank of vice admiral on April 11, 1951.

Following duty as Commander Amphibious Force, US Pacific Fleet, beginning on January 2, 1953, he reported on April 2, 1954 as Commander Naval Forces, Far East, serving there until September 14, 1956. He was Commander Western Sea Frontier from November 1956 until March 1, 1957 when he retired as a vice admiral after thirty-eight years of active duty.

Following his retirement, Callaghan served as the vice-president of American Export Lines, then as Chairman of the Maritime Transportation Research Board under the National Academy of Sciences. The transport ship GTS *Admiral W. M. Callaghan* is named in his honor.

Married three times and widowed twice, Callaghan had two children, the son, William M. Callaghan Jr. followed his father, graduating Annapolis, Class of 1949, serving as a naval aviator and retiring with the rank of rear admiral in 1980.

Callaghan retired to Chevy Chase, Maryland. He died following a stroke on July 8, 1991, at Bethesda Naval Hospital and he was buried at Arlington National Cemetery, beside his first two wives.

Callaghan's older brother, Rear Admiral Daniel J. Callaghan was killed in action on November 13, 1942 after a shell struck the bridge of his flagship, USS *San Francisco* (CA-38) during a surface action against a larger Japanese force off Savo Island, during the Guadalcanal campaign.

For his actions that day, Daniel Callaghan was awarded the Medal of Honor. The citation read:

"Although out-balanced in strength and numbers by a desperate and determined enemy, Rear Admiral Callaghan, with ingenious tactical skill and superb coordination of the units under his command, led his forces into battle against tremendous odds, thereby contributing decisively to the rout of a powerful invasion fleet and to the consequent frustration of a formidable Japanese offensive. While faithfully directing close-range operations in the face of furious bombardment by superior enemy fire power, he was killed on the bridge of his Flagship. His courageous initiative, inspiring leadership, and judicious foresight in a crisis of grave responsibility were in keeping with the finest traditions of the United States Naval Service. He gallantly gave his life in the defense of his country."

Captain Stuart S. Murray

When Captain Murray took command of *Missouri* on May 14, 1945, the war in Europe was over and the war in the Pacific was in its final stages, although the necessity of an invasion of the Japanese home islands, and the anticipated casualties loomed like dark clouds on the horizon.

Murray was an unusual choice considering that the overwhelming majority of his service was aboard submarines but his brief tenure in command would steer *Missouri* through the last months of the war, and more importantly, he would play a significant role in bringing the war to an end.

Stuart Shadrick Murray was born in Delia, Texas on March 22, 1898 and grew up in Texas and Oklahoma where his father was a former Mayor of Oklahoma City. Murray's brother. Clive, was already a Marine when he was appointed to the US Naval Academy from Oklahoma on June 8, 1915. He was on the rowing team and made the 1916 Summer Cruise aboard the USS *Wisconsin* (BB-9).

Because of the United States' entry into WW I in April 1917, the USNA Class of 1919 graduated early on June 6, 1918. Murray and six others had volunteered for the Marine Corps, and all seven applications were accepted, but forty-eight hours before graduation, all seven were called to the Office of the Commandant of Midshipmen to initial an order from Secretary of the Navy, Josephus Daniels. The order informed them that due to the need for line officers, they would be commissioned ensigns in the US Navy.

Murray's first assignment was to the Submarine School at New London Connecticut where he learned the basics of undersea warfare. There was no formal school and 18 weeks of training was conducted aboard the USS R-20 (SS-97) and USS R-17 (USS 94) and Murray qualified as a submariner on November 15, 1918.

In 1919, Murray met Madeleine Young, a beautiful young woman whom he married in 1921. They would have two children together, a daughter, Suzanne and a son. Stuart S. Murray Jr. who would graduate Annapolis in 1947 and retire as a lieutenant commander.

Murray was assigned aboard submarine, USS R-20 (SS-97) an R-class coastal and harbor defense submarine, on October 26, 1918 with Lieutenant Commander Alfred E. Montgomery in command.

Reporting aboard at San Pedro, California, the R-20 remained off southern California operating between San Pedro and San Diego, until March 1919 when she moved to San Francisco where she underwent overhaul, and on June 17, R-20, part of Submarine Division 14 (R-15 through R-20) as well as the tender USS Beaver, departed San Francisco for Hawaii. They arrived at Pearl Harbor on June 25.

Records indicate that Murray was involved in the construction of the submarine base at Pearl Harbor while also being promoted to Lt.(jg) and in March 1920 taking command of USS R-17 (SS-94). In May 1920, Commander Chester Nimitz replaced Commander Felix Gycax.

In the 1921 Murray got experience aboard battleships, serving on the USS *Arkansas* (BB-33) and in early 1921, *Arkansas* visited Valparaíso, Chile, where she was received by President Arturo Alessandri Palma; the ship's crew manned the rail to honor the Chilean president. In August 1921, *Arkansas* returned to the Atlantic Fleet, where she became the flagship of the Commander, Battleship Force, Atlantic Fleet.

In 1922, Murray transferred to USS *New York* (BB-34) operating with the Pacific Fleet conducting training and control duties, and he served as an instructor at the Naval Academy in the late 1920's and commanded the submarine USS S-34 (SS-155)

In mid-1933, Lieutenant Murray reported to the Portsmouth Naval Yard as assistant shop superintendent running the inside shops but within three months, he switched to assistant machinery superintendent working on the waterfront under Lt. Cmdr. Merrill Comstock.

While at Portsmouth, he helped develop the USS *Porpoise* (SS-172), the first of a new class of submarines that developed into the successful WW II fleet boats, driven by 4 diesel-electric drive engines. Porpoise was launched on June 20 and commissioned on August 15, 1935, Lieutenant Commander Stuart S. Murray in command.

After her shakedown cruise, *Porpoise* transited the Panama Canal and joined the Pacific Fleet at San Diego on September 1, 1936. After gunnery and torpedo practice off the west coast of the United States, she participated in Fleet Problem XVIII in the Hawaiian area, April–May 1937, and toward the end of the year underwent extensive overhaul at Mare Island Navy Yard.

Murray left the *Porpoise* in June 1937 to report aboard the cruiser USS *Portland* (CA-33) as the damage control officer. The *Portland* operated with the Scouting Force, Cruiser Division 5, in the Atlantic Ocean conducting peacetime training and a number of goodwill missions.

On January 1, 1939, Murray reported to the Bureau of Navigation assigned as detail officer for submarines, promoted to full commander on February 13, 1939 where he remained until July 1, 1940.

On November 1, 1940, he took command of Submarine Division 15 at San Diego. In October 1941 Submarine Division 15 was stationed in Manila, Philippines, which was the home of the Asiatic Fleet. Along with Cmdr. Joseph Connolly's Submarine Division 16 (SUBDIV16) Division 15 made up the entirety of Submarine Squadron

U.S.S. MISSOURI

2 (SUBRON2), under the command of Captain Walter Doyle, Commander Submarines Asia (COMSUBASIA)

After the Japanese attacked the Philippines in December 1941, and the situation worsened. Murray relocated into the tunnels of Corregidor on Christmas Day along with the top staff of Commander Submarine Asia, or everyone who had not fled earlier aboard the tender USS *Canopus* (AS-9).

Admiral Wilkes ordered all submarine crews out of the Philippines and on the evening of January 1, 1942, Murray boarded the USS *Swordfish* (SS-193) with Admiral Wilkes and others, to join Admiral Thomas C. Hart and the remains of the fleet in Surabaya, East Java.

After fleeing the Philippines, Hart pulled Murray's boats back to Fremantle, Western Australia, in compliance with Navy Department instructions. In Australia, Murray came under the command of his old boss from Submarine Division 13, Rear Admiral Charles Lockwood's Task Force 51, becoming chief of staff of Submarine Squadron 2, under Captain Jimmy Fife, also one of Lockwood's old Division 13 skippers. Murray was promoted to Captain on June 17, 1942.

With the death of Rear Admiral Robert H. English on January 21, 1943, Lockwood was named Commander Submarines Pacific, taking Murray along as his Chief of Staff, against the protests of the Commander Submarines Southwest Pacific.

In December 1943, Murray was ordered home to the US and was named Commandant of Midshipmen at Annapolis. Among the midshipmen at the Academy during Murray's time there were future president Jimmy Carter and future vice admiral and Medal of Honor recipient James B. Stockdale, as well as Murray's son, Stuart S. Murray Jr., Class of 1947.

On May 14, 1945, Murray returned to the Pacific to take command of the *Missouri*. On May 18, Admiral William F. Halsey Jr., the commander of Third Fleet, came aboard the ship, making her his fleet flagship. On May 21, *Missouri* got underway bound for Okinawa. She had reached the operational area by May 27, when she took part in attacks on Japanese positions on the island. She and the rest of Third Fleet then steamed north to conduct a series of air strikes on Japanese airfields and other installations on the island of Kyūshū on June 2 and 3 June.

The fleet was struck by a major typhoon on the night of June 5–6, which caused minor damage to *Missouri*. Another round of air strikes against targets on Kyūshū took place on June 8. The fleet then withdrew, sailing to Leyte Gulf to replenish fuel and ammunition, arriving there on June 13.

Underway again on July 8, the Third Fleet sailed to launch another series of attacks on the Japanese Home Islands. Carrier aircraft struck targets around Tokyo two days later, and then further north between Honshū and Hokkaidō from July 13 to 14. The following day, *Missouri* and several other vessels were detached to bombard industrial facilities in Muroran, Hokkaido. A second bombardment mission followed on the night of July 17/18 July before returning to cover the carriers during strikes against targets around the Inland Sea and then Tokyo later in the month.

After a brief pause, the carriers resumed attacks on northern Japan on August 9, the same day as the atomic bomb was dropped on Nagasaki. The following day, rumors circulated that Japan would surrender, which was formally announced on the morning of August 15. The next day, Admiral Sir Bruce Fraser of the Royal Navy, the Commander of the British Pacific Fleet, came aboard *Missouri* to confer the Knight Grand Cross of the Order of the British Empire on Halsey for his role in the war.

Murray was responsible for the preparations for the signing of the Japanese surrender. Japan officially surrendered to the Allies on August 15, but several weeks of preparation were necessary to amass the occupation forces and bring together the principal actors in one location for the official ceremony. The event was overseen by General of the Army Douglas MacArthur, who was named commander of Allied forces in occupied Japan, and his naval counterpart, Admiral Chester Nimitz.

President Harry Truman, although he did not attend, insisted that the battleship *Missouri,* named for his home state, be the venue for the surrender. Other ships had been considered, including the battle-tested carrier *Yorktown* and *Missouri*'s sister ship *Iowa*, as the *Missouri* had only been in the war for a little over a year. But Truman had attended its launch from the Brooklyn Navy Yard in January 1944, and his daughter Margaret had christened it and so the ship would be a stand-in for the president.

The crew of the *Missouri* was advised of this special honor only a few days before the ceremony. With no time to make a port call, all preparations had to be done at sea, including repainting decks and bulkheads; despite the fact that paint, being highly flammable, was strictly prohibited aboard Navy ships. Once the roster of attendees was known, sailors stood in for the dignitaries, practicing the movements of the ceremony down to the second.

One unlucky sailor even had to use a mop handle shoved down his pants to imitate the movements of the Japanese foreign minister, Mamoru Shigemitsu, who had a wooden leg.

When Missouri sailed into Tokyo Bay, it was accompanied by a flotilla of more than 250 Allied ships, including vessels of the British, Australian, and New Zealand navies. Additionally, ships of the Japanese Imperial Navy were present, their guns lowered and visibly plugged in a signal of surrender.

Of this vast armada, only two ships had been present at Pearl Harbor, the battleship West Virginia, (BB-48) and the cruiser Detroit (Cl -8) as well as the battleship South Dakota (BB-57) which had undergone a two-month overhaul at the Yard after nearly being sunk at Guadalcanal.

Among General MacArthur's demands for the ceremony were that his ensign, the flag of a five-star general, be flown from Missouri at the same height as also-five-star Adm. Nimitz' flag, requiring the welding of an additional flagpole onto the ship's topmast. But MacArthur also insisted that another flag be present for the ceremony, one that had been brought to Japan 92 years earlier.

In November 1852, Commodore Matthew C. Perry had set out from Norfolk, VA as commander of the East India Squadron. Aboard his flagship, the paddle-wheel steam frigate *Mississippi,* he carried a letter from President Millard Fillmore, addressed to the Emperor of Japan.

Perry's mission was to deliver this letter and open diplomatic and trade relations with a country that had been almost completely closed to outside contact for more than 200 years.

Perry's fleet, dubbed the "Black Ships," much smaller than the Allied force in 1945, entered Tokyo Bay in July 1853, where they were greeted with great suspicion and interest. After several days of negotiations with local officials and representatives of the ruling Tokugawa Shogunate, the real power in Japan behind the figurehead emperor, Perry and a force of 400 sailors and marines were finally allowed ashore to present their letter to the Japanese.

Rather than wait for an immediate response, Perry took his ships to Hong Kong, then returned in February 1854 to commence six weeks of talks and demonstrations of American power, after which Japan agreed to allow American ships to trade with Japan, to furnish US Navy ships with fuel and provisions, and to provide safe harbor to American vessels in distress.

The Treaty of Kanagawa marked the end of Japan's 220-year-old period of isolation and positioned the United States as an up-and-coming Pacific power. Shortly after his return to America, Commodore Perry presented the 31-starred American flag from his expedition to the US Naval Academy in Annapolis, where it was put on display.

MacArthur believed that it would be a fitting artifact to display aboard the *Missouri,* especially considering that Perry was a distant relative. A courier brought the flag from Annapolis, reportedly taking five days.

Other, more subtle arrangements were made. The Japanese delegates would pass between "sideboys", enlisted sailors who stand at attention on the quarterdeck as an honor to arriving dignitaries. The officer choosing the sideboys making sure that each towered above 6 feet, standing well above the diminutive Japanese.

The original plan called for General of the Army Douglas MacArthur to sign for all the Allied powers, which didn't set well with the US Navy which had borne the brunt of the Pacific war. Now, it wanted a slice of the glory and would represent the United State and

U.S.S. MISSOURI

MacArthur the Allies. On the gray overcast morning of Sept. 2, 1945, Japanese delegates filed aboard the *Missouri*.

The Japanese party arrived on time, shortly before 9 a.m., but Japanese Foreign Minister Mamoru Shigemitsu didn't arrive on the veranda deck until 9:03. General *MacArthur* stepped before a battery of microphones and opened the 23-minute surrender in which he made the connection between Perry's visit and the American return to Tokyo Bay in his remarks at the surrender ceremony, stating:

"We stand in Tokyo today, reminiscent of our countryman, Commodore Perry, 92 years ago. His purpose was to bring to Japan an era of enlightenment and progress by lifting the veil of isolation to the friendship, trade, and commerce of the world. But alas, the knowledge thereby gained of Western science was forged into an instrument of oppression and human enslavement. We are gathered here, representatives of the major warring powers, to conclude a solemn agreement whereby peace may be restored.

The issues, involving divergent ideals and ideologies, have been determined on the battlefields of the world and hence are not for our discussion or debate. Nor is it for us here to meet, representing as we do a majority of the people of the Earth, in a spirit of distrust, malice or hatred....

Photo # SC 210644   Spectators at Japanese surrender, 2 Sept. 1945

It is my earnest hope and indeed the hope of all mankind that from this solemn occasion a better world shall emerge out of the blood and carnage of the past

- a world founded upon faith and understanding - a world dedicated to the dignity of man and the fulfillment of his most cherished wish, for freedom, tolerance and justice. As supreme commander for the Allied powers, I announce it my firm purpose, in the tradition of the countries I represent, to proceed in the discharge of my responsibilities with justice and tolerance. Let us pray that peace now be restored to the world and that God will preserve it always. These proceedings are now closed."

With that, MacArthur put an arm around the shoulder of Admiral William "Bull" Halsey and whispered "*Start 'em now.*" His words triggered an order to orbiting warplanes and Navy fighters and Army Air Forces B-29s, hundreds of them, wave after wave, flew over the *Missouri* just as the sun broke through the overcast sky.

Some sources have claimed that the US flag raised over the *Missouri* was the flag which had flown over the U.S. Capitol on December 7, 1941. In fact, it was a flag taken from the ship's stock, according to Captain Murray' who in his memoirs, stated that it was "*just a plain ordinary GI-issue flag.*"

Murray was awarded two Legion of Merit Medals for his service during WW II. One for:

"his service as Chief of Staff for the Commander Submarine Force, Pacific Fleet, from 1 May 1943 to 16 November 1943" and a second award for "*the*

performance of outstanding services to the Government of the United States as Commanding Officer of the U.S.S. MISSOURI (BB-63), in operations against the Japanese from 6 March 1945 to 11 August 1945".

On November 6, 1945, Captain Roscoe H. Hillenkoetter, relieved Murray to take command of the *Missouri*. That same month, Murray was promoted to the rank of rear admiral and selected as Commander Seventh Fleet for duty with the U.S. Advisory Group to China.

With the end of a common Japanese enemy in China, the escalating fighting between the nationalists and communists for control threatened American marines serving in-country.

The War and Navy Departments in Washington feuded about the mechanics of a proposed US military advisory group that had been requested by the Nationalists at the end of August 1945. In a plan put forward on October 5, General Marshall put forward a plan that envisioned a combined army-navy advisory group that would be under the operational command and control of an army general who would report directly to the Joint Chiefs of Staff (JCS) and serve as the United States' chief military advisor to the Chinese Nationalist Government.

Admiral King completely rejected Marshall's proposal on grounds that it permitted the navy insufficient freedom, broke the navy's direct access to the Nationalist government, and reduced the navy to a secondary role. King counter proposed that two independent army and navy missions be sent, with a chairman to coordinate activities rather than to command and control. King's view, supported by Leahy, prevailed at a meeting of the JCS on October 27

In October and into November, American support was focused on helping its loyal wartime ally, the Nationalist Chinese, reoccupy territory lost to the Japanese, and mitigate the threat to Marines in direct confrontation with insurgent communist Chinese forces seeking to occupy the same areas.

In addition, there were ominous, unconfirmed reports of Soviets turning over captured Japanese arms to Chinese communist forces and other Soviet violations of agreements reached in the Sino-Soviet Friendship Treaty, and a fear that the Soviets intended to occupy Manchuria indefinitely or to establish a permanent sphere of influence through the use of Chinese communist surrogates. However, the Soviet "threat" was perceived differently between the military and civilian diplomats leading to a confusing and often ambiguous policy with regards to China

Murray had originally been scheduled to take over Naval Group China in December, but Vice Admiral Charles Maynard Cooke, who would serve as the naval consultant to the Republic of China's leader, Generalissimo Chiang Kai-shek, wanted to utilize Murray's outstanding organizational skills in a different way.

During a November 1945 meeting in Washington, D.C., Cooke informed Murray that Naval Group China, and the Sino-American Cooperation Association (SACO) would be shut down and he would instead take over the Qingdao naval training program and the newly created Naval Assistance Group to China. Murray thus had the dual responsibilities of training the new Chinese Navy and overseeing the transfer of U.S. Navy ships and resources.

Murray's official orders authorized him to form a preliminary administrative Survey Board for the purposes of establishing a long term Naval Advisory Group in China and determining the realistic requirements to build and train a Chinese Navy and to report his findings to Cooke.

Throughout December, Murray and his staff surveyed Chinese port facilities and observed the general state of the Chinese Navy and Murray met with Chinese officials in Canton and on the island of Formosa regarding the future needs and plans of the Chinese Navy.

The promise of sending additional troops to Manchuria, along with the establishment of the training center at Tsingtao and the actions of Murray's Naval Survey Group encouraged the Nationalists to assume that they really enjoyed the full support of the United States and could thus enter into superficial agreements with the communists.

Because of the Nationalists' apparent willingness to negotiate a peaceful settlement to the civil war, Marshall gave his approval in principle to U. S. naval plans for an assistance mission to China then nearing completion in Washington and strongly recommended by Rear Admiral Murray and the new Commander of the Seventh Fleet, Admiral Cooke.

For the next three years, Murray worked trying to carry out a poorly defined and often contradictory mission. As Murray later recalled:

"We were operating now as advisors to the Chinese Navy even though we were unofficial in that we were not officially established. As far as the Chinese were concerned, it made no difference to them. We were just there and whether we were officially established or not had no bearing as far they were concerned. They wanted assistance."

From 1948 to 1949 Murray commanded the Pearl Harbor Naval Base, followed by assignment as the Commander Amphibious Training Command Atlantic Fleet (CATCUSAF) until 1950. From June 1, 1950, Murray served as Commander Submarine Force Atlantic Fleet (COMSUBLANT) with the responsibility to operate, maintain, train, and equip submarines. Murray was relieved by Rear Admiral George C. "Turkey Neck" Crawford on June 6, 1952, when Murray was appointed as Commandant of the 14th Naval District at Pearl Harbor, Hawaii

Relieved by Rear Admiral Clarence E. Olsen on February 18, 1954, Murray's final assignment was as Inspector General of the Navy, beginning in June 1954, operating out of Washington DC and he was promoted to Vice Admiral (3-stars) on December 7, 1955.

Murray retired from active duty in August 1956 after 37 years of continuous naval service and was promoted to full admiral upon his retirement. Following his retirement, Murray took work as a consultant on Anti-submarine warfare (ASW) and missile development for the Rand Corporation.

In 1974 Murray published his memoirs, "*The Reminiscences of Admiral Stuart S. Murray.*" He died in Washington DC on September 19, 1980, at the age of 82. He is buried at Arlington National Cemetery.

Captain Murray with President Truman signing the
U.S.S. Missouri Visitors Log

U.S.S. Missouri

Captain Roscoe H. Hillenkoetter

Possibly one of the most colorful figures in US Naval History, when Captain Hillenkoetter took command of the USS *Missouri* on November 6, 1945, his 6-month command would be a footnote in a career that patrolled the Atlantic during World War One, assisted the French Underground, survived the attack at Pearl Harbor, was instrumental in developing the American post-war intelligence network, fought in Korea, and investigated UFOs.

Roscoe Henry Hillenkoetter was born on May 8, 1897 in a German neighborhood of St. Louis, Missouri the only child of Alexander W. Hillenkoetter, a postal inspector and his French wife, Olinda du Ker.

Hillenkoetter was given an appointment to the US Naval Academy from the state of Missouri, entering on June 8, 1916. He was aboard the USS *Michigan* (BB-27) a Connecticut-class battleship, for the 1916 practice cruise. With America's entry into WW I, the academy midshipmen served at sea, and Hillenkoetter served aboard the USS *Minnesota* (BB-22) with the Atlantic Fleet on anti-submarine patrols.

Promoted to Midshipman Chief Petty Officer his senior year and ranked 20th in a class of 467, graduating with the rest of the Class of 1920 on June 6, 1919 and was commissioned an ensign in the US Navy the following day.

U.S.S. MISSOURI

Assigned aboard the USS *Bushnell* (AS-2) in June 1919, the ship was a submarine tender named for David Bushnell, inventor of the first American submarine and was commissioned on February 9, 1915.

In July 1920, Hillenkoetter was transferred to the USS S-7 (SS-112) which was launched on February 5, 1920 and commissioned on July 1, 1920 with Lieutenant Commander Sherwood Picking in command. USS S-7 sailed from New London, Connecticut on November 18, 1920 for Pearl Harbor but Hillenkoetter was not aboard, having transferred to the Dubuque-class gunboat USS *Paducah* (PG-18) in September 1920.

Commissioned on September 2, 1905, she served in the Caribbean and escorted convoys to North Africa, Italy, the Azores, and Madeira during WWI. She attacked a U-boat September 9, 1918 and is credited with damaging the submarine. Leaving Gibraltar on December 11, the *Paducah* reached Portsmouth, New Hampshire, on January 7, 1919, scheduled to be decommissioned on March 2, 1919.

Recommissioned on August 16, 1920 to perform survey duty in the Caribbean. *Paducah* was decommissioned again on September 9, 1921 and in October Hillenkoetter was assigned aboard the USS *Israel* (DD-98) a Wickes-class destroyer commissioned on September 13, 1918.

Sailing from Portsmouth, New Hampshire on March 4, 1921, *Israel* cruised along the East Coast until July 5 when she joined Mine Squadron 1, Atlantic Fleet, at Gloucester, Massachusetts. For the remainder of the year, she engaged in mining practice and exercises on the East Coast. From January until April 1922, she was part of fleet exercises based at Guantanamo Bay, Cuba and Culebra, Puerto Rico. *Israel* arrived in Philadelphia on May 15, 1922 and Hillenkoetter was promoted to lieutenant (jg)on June 7, 1922, just prior to *Israel* being decommissioned there on July 7.

From August through December 1922, Hillenkoetter took instruction at the submarine base at New London, Connecticut, then reported aboard the submarine USS O-2 (SS-63), a WWI era O-class submarine. Used as a training vessel, Hillenkoetter remained until December of 1923, when he reported to Balboa, Panama for shore duty with the 15th Naval District in the Canal Zone. In February 1925, he was appointed aide to Rear Admiral Noble E. Irwin, the

Commander 15th Naval District with a promotion to full lieutenant on June 7.

In October 1925, Hillenkoetter reported to the Norfolk Naval Base, Virginia for duty as an aide on the staff of the Commander – Destroyer Squadron Scouting Fleet in the Atlantic.

In July 1927, Hillenkoetter returned to Balboa, Panama for service on the staff of Rear Admiral David Foote Sellers, Commander Special Services Squadron. The squadron patrolled the Caribbean Sea as an instrument of gunboat diplomacy and was involved with sending Marines to occupy parts of Nicaragua when Civil war erupted between the conservative and liberal factions on May 2, 1926.

In 1928 Hillenkoetter first became involved in intelligence operations when he helped oversee elections in Nicaragua. President Herbert Hoover ordered American troops home on January 2, 1933, ending 21 years of US intervention in Nicaragua. In May 1929, Hillenkoetter reported to the Naval Academy assigned as an instructor in the Modern Languages Department. After a two-year term, he reported aboard the Omaha-class light cruiser USS *Memphis* (CL-13) in June 1931, Captain Joseph Vance Ogan in command.

His time aboard the Memphis was short, the ship and in December 1931, Hillenkooetter reported to the Philadelphia Navy yard to assist in the fitting out of the Clemson-class destroyer USS *Bainbridge* (DD-242)

On December 23, 1930 she had been placed out of commission in reserve at the Philadelphia yard and on March 9, 1932, the *Bainbridge* returned to the fleet in reduced commission and was attached to Rotating Reserve Division 19, taking part in Naval Reserve training cruises. Hillenkoetter served as both XO and engineering officer until May 1932.

In May 1932, Hillenkoetter was again sent to Nicaragua where he served during the Banana Wars and specifically the Second Nicaraguan Campaign. He was there to again help facilitate with the elections happening in Nicaragua at the time. For his actions in Nicaragua, he was presented the Nicaraguan Medal of Merit.

In December 1932, Hillenkoetter left Nicaragua to return to Panama and the staff of Commander Special Services Squadron, this time as Flag Lieutenant to Rear Admiral Arthur St. Clair Smith. In May of 1933, was upgraded to Flag Secretary until October when Hillenkoetter received orders sending him to France.

Hillenkoetter arrived at the US Embassy in Paris as the assistant naval attaché in late 1933. He remained in Paris until called home to the United States in September 1935, and the next month, he was assigned to the USS *Maryland* (BB-46).

Homeported in Long Beach, California, she patrolled the California coast. In his time aboard, Hillenkoetter served under two captains, Captain George Sloan Bryan (July 27, 1935 thru June 20, 1936) and Captain Louis P Davis (June 20, 1936 thru

USS MARYLAND BB-46

December 16, 1937), serving as gunnery officer towards the end of his tour, leaving the ship in February 1938.

In April 1938, he returned to the US Embassy in Paris as assistant naval attaché this time acting concurrently as the assistant naval attaché for Madrid, Spain and at the American Legation at Lisbon, Portugal.

During this period, tensions were high as the worldwide economic depression weakened western democracies and fascist governments came to power in Germany, Italy and Spain. On September 30, 1938, the Munich Agreement was signed by France, Germany, Britain, and Italy permitting German annexation of Czechoslovakia's Sudetenland.

There was a civil war in Spain from 1936 thru 1939, and Hillenkoetter assisted in evacuating American citizens. On July 1, 1939, Hillenkoetter was promoted to full commander and in April 1940, following the German invasion of Poland on September 1, 1939 initiating the start of the Second World War, he was named the Naval Attaché in Paris and relieved of his duties in Madrid and Lisbon.

After the German invasion of France, Hillenkoetter entered Vichy France and aided the underground movement, helping hunted fugitives escape occupied France. Having earlier set up a spy network in Panama, he became adept at gathering intelligence, skills that would serve him later on.

On August 30, 1941, Hillenkoetter returned to the United States, then departed to the Pacific to report aboard the Colorado-class battleship USS *West Virginia* (BB-48) as executive officer under Captain Mervyn Sharp Bennion.

The *West Virginia* was in port at Pearl Harbor on December 7, 1941, moored outboard of the USS *Tennessee* (BB-43) at berth F-6. Since the *West Virginia* was moored outboard, the ship was struck by several hits from seven Type 91 torpedoes on her port side, while bombers hit her with a pair of 16 in (410 mm) armor-piercing shells that had been converted into bombs.

The first bomb hit the port side and penetrated the superstructure deck, causing extensive damage to the casemates below. Secondary explosions of the ammunition stored in the casemates caused serious fires and it was only through the courageous and quick actions of the *West Virginia* crew was the ship prevented from capsizing like the USS *Oklahoma* (BB-37).

Captain Bennion was killed in action during the Japanese attack. Mortally wounded by a shrapnel shard from the nearby Tennessee after she was hit by a bomb, reportedly disemboweling him, he refused to leave his post, eventually ordering his men to leave him and abandon ship. Using one arm to hold his wounds closed, Bennion bled to death on the spot while still commanding his crew.

During the first wave of the attack, and during the counter-flooding operation overseen by Lt. Commander John S. Harper, the damage control officer, Hillenkoetter had abandoned ship by jumping off the starboard quarterdeck. Subsequently, Harper received notification from an officer on the conning tower that the captain was dying, the executive officer had abandoned ship, and as third in command, Harper was now the commanding officer.

After confirming that all starboard voids had been flooded, Harper proceeded to the conning tower and countermanded the captain's dying order for all hands to abandon ship. Instead, he ordered repair parties to fight fires fore and aft. Fire hoses from the *Tennessee* were passed to the *West Virginia*, and crews fought fires near gun turret 3 and elsewhere on the ship until about 2:00 pm, when Harper finally ordered the remaining crew to abandon ship.

West Virginia was abandoned, settling to the harbor bottom on an even keel, her fires fought from on board by a party that volunteered to return to the ship after the first abandonment. By the afternoon of the following day, December 8, the flames had been extinguished. With a patch over the damaged area of her hull, the battleship was later pumped out and ultimately refloated on May 17, 1942.

Captain Bennion was posthumously awarded the Medal of Honor. Hillenkoetter as the most senior surviving crewmember of the *West Virginia* directed efforts from the shore and later received the Purple Heart for injuries sustained during the attack.

On December 15, Hillenkoetter returned to the battleship *Maryland* as executive officer. The ship, which had been damaged in the attack, sailed to Puget Sound Navy Yard in Washington state on December 30. Repairs were completed on February 26, 1942. She then underwent a series of shakedown cruises to West Coast ports and the Christmas Islands before being sent back into action in June 1942, the second ship damaged at Pearl Harbor to return to duty. He was aboard when Maryland played a supporting role in the Battle of Midway, June 4-7, 1942.

Promoted to captain on June 18, 1942, Hillenkoetter was detached from the ship on July 3, 1942 and after a brief return to Washington, he returned to the Pacific, reporting in September 1942 as Officer in Charge (OIC) of the intelligence section on the staff of Admiral Chester W. Nimitz, Commander in Chief – Pacific.

Hillenkoetter left Nimitz's staff on March 28, 1943 to take command of the destroyer tender USS *Dixie* (AD-14) and served as acting Commander – Destroyers Pacific Fleet until February 1, 1944. For his service, he was awarded a Bronze Star Medal. The citation read:

CAPTAIN ROSCOE H. HILLENKOETTER

"For meritorious service in connection with operations against the enemy as Commanding Officer of a Destroyer Tender of the United States Navy from April 1943 to February 1944. Captain Hillenkoetter displayed able leadership, outstanding initiative and professional skill in tending a large number of Destroyers during the long and arduous Solomons campaign when their services were vital to our forces."

In February, Hillenkoetter was called back to Washington DC to serve in the Bureau of Naval Personnel serving first as Assistant Director of Training, and then as Director of Planning and Control, for which he was awarded the Legion of Merit Medal.

Following the end of the war, Hilllenkoetter took command of the USS *Missouri* in New York City, after relieving Captain Stuart S. Murray on November 7, 1945. The ship was fresh from carrying servicemen home as part of Operation *Red Carpet* and had arrived in New York City on October 23, 1945.

*Mi*ssouri was scheduled for an overhaul at the New York Navy Yard and Hillenkoetter's time in command would be brief, but not uneventful. Following her overhaul *Missouri* took a training cruise to Cuba, then returned to New York. On March 21, 1946, she received the remains of the Turkish Ambassador to the United States, Münir Ertegun.

Arriving at Gibraltar, Admiral Henry Kent Hewitt, the Commander of all United States Naval Forces in Europe, boarded the *Missouri* and completed the remainder of her cruise, escorted by the destroyer USS *Power* (DD-839) and the light cruiser USS *Providence* (CL-82).

The *Missouri* anchored at the Port of Bosphorus, off Istanbul, where the body of the ambassador was removed, firing a 19-gun salute during the transfer of the remains and again during the funeral ashore. *Missouri* departed Istanbul on April 9 and entered Phaleron Bay, Piraeus, Greece, the following day for an overwhelming welcome by Greek government officials and anti-communist citizens.

Greece was in the midst of a civil war between the Communist resistance movement of WW II and the returning Greek government-in-exile. The United States saw this as an important test case for its new doctrine of containment of the Soviet Union.

U.S.S. MISSOURI

Missouri made port calls at Pirawus, Naples, Algiers and Tangier and her voyage through the eastern Mediterranean symbolized America's strategic commitment to the region. The visit to Turkey was the first visit by a US warship since September 1930. During this cruise, Hillenkoetter was awarded the Order of the Phoenix, degree of Commander, by the Government of Greece, the presentation being made at Athens on April 10, 1946.

He was also awarded the Order of Saint Maurice and Saint Lazarus, degree of Commander, by' the Government of Italy, the presentation being made on April 22, 1946. The *Missouri* returned to Gibraltar and from there to the United States, arriving in Norfolk, Virginia on May 9, 1946.

Hillenkoetter was relieved of command of the *Missouri* by Captain Tom B. Hill on May 31, and on July 29, 1946, he reported to Paris, France, for another tour of duty there, this time as the Naval attaché with a promotion to rear admiral on November 29, 1946.

In May 1947, he was persuaded by President Harry S. Truman to become the third Director of Central Intelligence (DCI), and run the Central Intelligence Group (CIG) which had replaced the Office of Strategic Services (OSS) the wartime intelligence service. He replaced Lt. Gen. Hoyt Vandenberg as DCI. Under the National Security Act of 1947, Hillenkoetter was nominated and confirmed by the U.S. Senate as the first Director of the newly established Central Intelligence Agency.

It was a challenging assignment, and although he had experience in intelligence operations, he lacked experience in running a bureaucracy and growing international pressures put demands on the new agency that were difficult to meet. He found himself caught in the middle between Secretary of State Dean Acheson and Secretary of Defense Louis A. Johnson who had decidedly different views on policy. Nor was there necessarily good cooperation between Army and Naval Intelligence, and as only a rear admiral, he lacked leverage to compel their cooperation and often intelligence was not always shared.

Under Hillenkoetter's watch as DCI, the Soviets detonated an atomic bomb (August 29, 1949), and North Korean troops crossed over into South Korea (June 25, 1950), both events taking the CIA by surprise. Whether because of his desire to return to active naval service, or dissatisfaction with his job as CIA Director, Hillenkoetter was replaced by General Walter Bedell Smith, Gen. Eisenhower's wartime chief of staff, on October 7, 1950.

With the United States in an undeclared war in Korea and Rear Admiral Hillenkoetter returned to the navy in command of the cruiser USS *Saint Paul* (CA-73) which deployed to Korea in late July 1950.

Following the defeat of UN forces at the Battle of the Chosin Reservoir (November 27 thru December 13) by the Chinese People's Volunteer Army (PVA) in the Second Phase Campaign, UN forces retreated to Hungnam from where they were to be evacuated to South Korea.

Saint Paul commenced combat operations off the northeast coast of Korea on November 9. On November 17, she provided gunfire support to the UN troops advancing on Chongjin. That day, shrapnel from a near miss by a shell from a Communist shore battery injured six men at gun mount stations. The cruiser destroyed the enemy emplacement with counter-battery fire and continued her support mission.

As the Chinese Communists began massive attacks late in November, UN forces commenced a general withdrawal to consolidate and hold south of the 38th parallel. *Saint Paul* provided close support for the Republic of Korea (ROK) I Corps as they withdrew from Hapsu, and along the coast to Chongjin.

Following the defeat of UN forces at the Battle of the Chosin Reservoir (November 27 thru December 13) by the Chinese People's Volunteer Army (PVA) in the Second Phase Campaign, UN forces retreated to Hungnam from where they were to be evacuated to South Korea.

Hillenkoetter commanded Task Group 90.8 (TG-90.8) the Gunfire Support Group, part of Task Force 90 under the command of Rear Admiral J.H. Doyle. TG 90.8 consisted of the cruiser USS *Saint Paul*, Hillenkoetter's flagship, Destroyer Division 162 comprised of four destroyers, USS *Massey* (DD-778), USS *Zellers* (DD-777), USS *Speery* (DD-697) and USS *Forrest Royal* (DD-872) as well as 3 LSM(R) 401, 403 and 404 (Landing Ship Medium – Rocket). In addition, his force was supplemented by the cruiser USS *Rochester* (CA-124) and a destroyer detached from Rear Admiral J. A. Higgins TG-95.2

Saint Paul entered the harbor at Wonsan on December 3 to provide a curtain of shellfire around that city as United Nations forces, and equipment was moved to Hungnam and Saint Paul remained to cover the evacuation of that city and harbor between December 10 and 24.

By the time the evacuation was nearing completion on December 24, Hillenkoetter's force included the battleship *Missouri* and an additional three destroyers. From December 7-24, TG-90.8 warships fired 162 rounds of 16-inch, 2,932 rounds of 8-inch, 18,637 rounds of 5-inch, 71 rounds of 3-inch, 185 rounds of 40-mm and 1,462 rockets.

From January 21-31, 1951, *Saint Paul* conducted shore bombardment missions north of Inchon where, on January 26, she was again fired upon by shore batteries. On April 7, in TF 74, *Saint Paul* helped to carry out raids on rail lines and tunnels utilizing 250 commandos of the 41st Independent Royal Marines.

Saint Paul returned home for yard work at San Francisco, California, from June to September, then conducted underway training before sailing for Korea on November 5. She arrived off Wonsan on November 27 and began gun strike missions in support of the UN blockade.

During the following weeks, she bombarded strategic points at Hungnam, Songjin, and Chongjin. In December, she served as an anti-aircraft escort for TF 77, and, following a holiday trip to Japan, resumed operations off the coast of North Korea.

In April 1952, *Saint Paul* participated in combined air-sea attacks against the ports of Wonsan and Chongjin. On April 21, while the cruiser was engaged in gun fire support operations, 30 men were killed a gun in the forward turret blew up.

Despite the loss, *Saint Paul* carried out gun strikes on railroad targets near Songjin and captured nine North Koreans from a small boat before returning to Japan for repairs. Following a brief stay in port and two weeks on the gun line, she departed for home and reached Long Beach, California, on June 24, 1952.

Captain Roscoe H. Hillenkoetter

Detached from the *Saint Paul* in June, Hillenkoetter was named Commandant of the 3rd Naval District in New York with the concurrent duty as Commandant of the Brooklyn Navy Yard in July, and he was promoted to vice admiral on April 9, 1956, just prior to being relieved by Rear Admiral Milton Miles in August.

His last assignment was as the Navy's Inspector General, from August 1, 1956, until his retirement on May 1, 1957, after 38 years of continuous military service. After his retirement, he served on the National Investigations Committee on Aerial Phenomena from 1957 until 1962 and he sought public disclosure of UFO evidence.

Retiring to Weehawken, New Jersey, he passed away at Mount Sinai Hospital in New York on June 18, 1982 from heart complications and emphysema at the age of 85. On June 24, 1982, Admiral Hillenkoetter was buried with full military honors at Arlington National Cemetery.

U.S.S. MISSOURI

Captain Tom B. Hill

Captain Tom Hill is present in one of the most iconic photographs of the Twentieth Century yet is hardly noticeable standing behind figures such as Macarthur, Nimitz and Halsey during the Japanese surrender aboard the deck of the USS *Missouri* on September 2, 1945. He is just behind the first row of officers witnessing the surrender.

Eight months later, on May 31, 1946, he would take command of the *Missouri* after which he would help guide the US Navy into the nuclear age.

TOM BURBRIDGE HILL

Tom Burbridge Hill was born in Fort Worth, Texas on December 12, 1898, the only child of Benjamin Felix and Norma Hill. He was appointed to the US Naval Academy from the state of Texas on June 15, 1918.

Hill took his summer cruise aboard the USS *Connecticut* (BB-18) and was selected as Midshipman Ensign for his class, graduating 141 in a class of 540 on June 2, 1922 and was commissioned an ensign in the US Navy. His first assignment was to the USS *Idaho* (BB-42) a New Mexico-class battleship commissioned in March 1919.

Idaho operated in the Pacific Fleet, conducting maneuvers and routine training exercises and he learned the duties of a naval officer at sea. In 1924, he was sent for instruction to the Naval Air Station (NAS) Pensacola, Florida

U.S.S. MISSOURI

On November 10, 1924, Hill received orders to report aboard the battleship USS *Nevada* (BB-36) and took part in the US Fleet's "goodwill cruise" to Australia and New Zealand, from July through September 1925. During this cruise, the ships had only limited replenishment opportunities, but demonstrated to those allies and Japan that the US Navy had the ability to conduct transpacific operations.

In May 1928, he was one of only three graduates of the Naval Postgraduate School to be selected to attend the University of Michigan to earn a master's degree in explosives engineering.

From 1930 to 1932, Hill, now a lieutenant, was assigned aboard the USS *Medusa* (AR-1) the Navy's first purpose-built repair ship. *Meedusa* was homeported out of San Pedro, California, operating with the Pacific Fleet *Medusa* was capable of blacksmith work, boiler repairs, carpentry, copper-smithing, electrical work, foundry work, pipe work, plating, sheet-metal work, welding, and repairs of optical and mechanical equipment. Her machinery shop's equipment included lathes, radial drills, milling machines, slotting machines, boring machines, optical repair equipment, armature bake ovens, and coil winding machines. To meet additional demands from the fleet, she had a motion picture shop, large laundry and bakery facilities, and large refrigeration units.

From 1934-35, Hill was assigned as assistant inspector at Bausch and Lowe Optical, Rochester, New York and in 1936, he returned to sea duty assigned aboard the battleship USS *California* (BB-44). During his time aboard, he was promoted to lt. commander.

Part of the Pacific Battle Fleet, in mid-1937, *California* transferred to Battleship Division 2, and on July 7, the ships of the division visited Hawaii, returning to California on August 22. *California* and her sister *Tennessee* transited the Panama Canal in early 1938 for a visit to Ponce, Puerto Rico, which lasted from March 6 to 11.

After shore duty as Inspector of Naval Material at Schenectady, New York, Hill helped fit out the USS *North Carolina* (BB-55) at the New York Naval Shipyard where he reported aboard as the gunnery officer, with a promotion to full commander upon her commissioning on April 9, 1941, under the command of Captain Olaf M. Hustvedt. *North Carolina* embarked on her shakedown cruise in the Caribbean Sea and spent the rest of the year working up, while the United States remained neutral during World War II.

Following the Japanese attack on Pearl Harbor on December 7, *North Carolina* began extensive battle training to prepare for combat in the Pacific. On April 23, 1942, she was deployed to Naval Station Argentina as part of a force intended to block a potential sortie by the German battleship *Tirpitz* if she attempted to break out into the convoy lanes of the North Atlantic. *Tirpitz* remained in Norway, and North Carolina was quickly replaced by the battleship *South Dakota*, allowing *North Carolina* to get underway for the Pacific in mid-1942.

She passed through the Panama Canal on June 10 in company with the aircraft carriers USS *Wasp* (CV-7) and USS *Long Island* (CVE-1) and nine destroyers. On June 15, *North Carolina* was assigned to Rear Admiral Leigh Noye's Task Force 18 (TF-18), comprised of the USS *Wasp*, along with four cruisers and nine destroyers.

Assigned to strengthen Allied naval forces during the battle for Guadalcanal, *North Carolina* screened aircraft carriers engaged in the campaign and took part in the Battle of the Eastern Solomons on August 24-25, where she shot down several Japanese aircraft. As an action report stated:

"On August 24, 1942, this ship engaged in repelling a coordinated air attack by Japanese planes on Task Force Sixteen... The reports of observers indicate that the Enterprise and the North Carolina were the principal objectives of the attack of about forty (40) enemy aircraft. The action was notable for the large number of planes reaching bombing attack points and the enormous volume of anti-aircraft fire. The *North Carolina* suffered no structural damage in spite of seven (7) near-miss bombs and some strafing. The casualties amounted to one (1) killed (enlisted) and none wounded."

The next month, she was torpedoed by a Japanese submarine but was not seriously damaged. After repairs, she returned to the campaign and continued to screen carriers during the campaigns across the central Pacific in 1943 and 1944.

In the summer of 1944, Hill, now a captain, was assigned to the staff of Admiral Chester W. Nimitz, the Commander in Chief – Pacific (CINCPAC) as the commanding the Combat Readiness Division. As such, he was the only staff member brought into the Manhattan Project by Nimitz.

As part of Nimitz's staff, Hill was present on deck during the Japanese surrender ceremony aboard the USS *Missouri* in Tokyo Bay on September 2, 1945. The *Missouri* was anchored as close to the spot where Commodore Perry had anchored his flagship as Hillenkoetter could manage.

On May 31, 1946, Hill took command of the *Missouri* in New York City and spent the next year operating in Atlantic coastal waters conducting a number of command training exercises.

On December 13, 1946, engaged in a target practice exercise in the North Atlantic, a star shell accidentally struck the battleship, but without causing injuries. On April 2, 1947, Hill turned command over to Captain Robert L. Dennison.

After temporary duty at Oak Ridge, Tennessee, Hill was the Sr. Naval Officer for Operation *Sandstone* in 1948. Operation *Sandstone* was the third series of American nuclear tests, following *Trinity* in 1945 and *Crossroads* in 1946, and preceding *Ranger*. Like the *Crossroads* tests, the *Sandstone* tests were carried out at the Pacific Proving Grounds, although at Enewetak Atoll rather than Bikini Atoll. They differed from Crossroads in that they were conducted by the Atomic Energy Commission, with the armed forces having only a supporting role.

Sandstone was actually three tests, *X-Ray* on April 14, *Yoke* on April 30 and *Zebra* on May 14, 1948 and was carried out by a work force of 10,366 personnel, of whom 9,890 were military.

In January 1949, Hill was assigned to the Office of Chief of Naval Operations with a promotion to rear admiral. In July, Hill was named the Navy Director of Atomic Energy and military liaison to the Atomic Energy Commission.

On July 11, 1949, Hill, replaced Admiral William S. Parsons as Deputy Chief of AFSWP, the Armed Forces Special Weapons Project which was the United States military agency responsible for those aspects of nuclear weapons remaining under military control after the Manhattan Project was succeeded by the Atomic Energy Commission on January 1, 1947.

These responsibilities included the maintenance, storage, surveillance, security and handling of nuclear weapons, as well as supporting nuclear testing. The AFSWP was a joint organization, staffed by the United States Army, United States Navy and United States Air Force; its chief was supported by deputies from the other two services.

In June 1950, Hill returned to the naval academy, teaching a course in International Relations. On January 25, 1951, Rear Admiral Hill, who had been director of the Navy's Atomic Energy Division, was named deputy director of Joint Task Force 3, the force was responsible for atomic weapons projects in the central Pacific. JTF-3 was formed in late 1949 in preparation for Operation *Greenhouse* nuclear test series.

Promoted to the permanent rank of rear admiral, Hill was again the Sr. Naval Officer present for Operation *Greenhouse* in April-May 1951.

Operation *Greenhouse* was the fifth American nuclear test series, the second conducted in 1951 and the first to test principles that would lead to developing thermonuclear weapons (hydrogen bombs). Conducted again at the new Pacific Proving Ground, on islands of the Enewetak Atoll, all of the devices were mounted in large steel towers, to simulate air bursts.

It consisted of four tests, *Dog* on April 7, *Easy* on April 20, *George* on May 8, and *Item* on May 24, 1951. Operation *Greenhouse* showcased new and aggressive designs for nuclear weapons. The main idea was to reduce the size, weight, and most importantly, reduce the amount of fissile material necessary for nuclear weapons, while increasing the destructive power.

On January 25, 1951 Hill, was relieved as the director of the Navy's Atomic Energy Division and was named deputy director of

Joint Task Force 3, responsible for atomic weapons projects in the central Pacific.

On September 3, 1951, Rear Admiral Hill, Commander Amphibious Group 1, relieved Vice Admiral I. N. Kiland as Commander Amphibious Force Far East, but after only a brief time in command, on October 13, Vice Admiral Carl F. Espe relieved Rear Admiral Hill as Commander Amphibious Group One (COMPHIBGRU1).

From October 1951 until August 1952, Hill served as chief of staff to the Commander in Chief -Pacific (CINCPAC) Admiral Arthur W. Radford. In July 1954, Hill was named Commandant of Potomac River Naval Command in Washington DC., known today as Naval District Washington.

Hill was married to Lillian Mary Louise Jamison Hill with whom he had two children, Norma Lillian Redfield and a son, Thomas Burbridge Hill Jr. who served as a naval officer during WW II and died on the tenth anniversary of the attack on Pearl Harbor, December 7, 1951.

L-R CAPTAIN TOM B. HILL, REAR ADMIRAL THORVALD SOLBERG and REAR ADMIRAL WILLIAM PARSONS OAK RIDGE, TENNESSEE 1947.

Hill retired from the navy as a vice admiral in 1955, and moved to Bethesda, Maryland where he passed away on October 22, 1957 at the age of 58. He was buried with full military honors in Section 2, Site 4969C.

CAPTAIN TOM B. HILL

U.S.S. Missouri

Captain Robert L. Dennison

Of the twenty men who commanded the USS *Missouri*, Robert Dennison operated at the highest levels of government and was involved in some of the most significant events of the 20th Century.

His close relationships with many prominent individuals include Nimitz, MacArthur, Eisenhower, Churchill as well as Presidents Kennedy and Truman.

Robert Lee Dennison was born in Warren, Pennsylvania on April 13, 1901 to Ludovici Waters Dennison and Laura Florence Lee and he grew up in northwestern Pennsylvania. He attended Kiskiminetas Preparatory School before being admitted to the US Naval Academy on June 18, 1919.

He was aboard the USS *New Hampshire* (BB-25) for the 1920 practice cruise and the cruiser USS *South Dakota* (AC-9) in 1921. He graduated 83rd in a class of 414 and graduated with a commission as an ensign on June 7, 1923. A classmate was future admiral Arleigh Burke.

Dennison's first assignment was to the USS *Arkansas* (BB-33), a Wyoming-class battleship commissioned in September 1912.

During World War I, she was part of Battleship Division Nine, which was attached to the British Grand Fleet, but she saw no action during the war. In the early 1920's she was used primarily to train midshipmen and for goodwill visits.

In 1925, Dennison reported to the submarine school at New London Navy Yard, Groton, Connecticut where he was promoted to lieutenant (jg) and after qualifying as a submariner, he was assigned to the submarine USS S-8 (SS-113)

The S-8 operated along the West Coast through February 1927, when she was sent to Coco Solo, Panama Canal Zone, for a few months, then continued on to New London, Connecticut. For the remainder of her active service she was based in New England, but made training voyages to Panama in 1928, 1929 and 1930. In April 1931 USS S-8 was taken out of commission. When Dennison left the S-8 in 1930, it was with the rank of lieutenant.

Dennison reported aboard the heavy cruiser USS Chester (CA-27) commissioned on June 24, 1930, Captain Arthur P. Fairfield in command.

USS CHESTER (CA-27) CIRCA 1930

Chester steamed to New York Navy Yard, Brooklyn, N.Y. arriving July 7 where she received her first aircraft, Vought O2U 3 *Corsairs*, as well as ammunition and stores. She departed August 7 and the following day, Lt. James R. Tague and AMM2c Alvin Brinkley became the first aircrew to launch from *Chester*.

On August 13, she set out for Barcelona, Spain and passed through the Strait of Gibraltar, arriving at Barcelona on August 25. After making a port call to Naples, Italy, September 2-11, Chester set out for Istanbul, Turkey. on 11 September. Shortly after leaving port they learned from radio that Mount Stromboli, a volcano on the Italian island of the same name had erupted.

Chester's course passed near Stromboli, so Captain Fairfield sent a message to the Italian government asking if his ship could be of any assistance but received a message that assistance was not required. Before she arrived at Turkey, Fairfield received a personal message from Italian Prime Minister Benito Mussolini thanking him for the captain's offer.

Chester arrived at Istanbul on September 15, then sailed to Athens on September 22, followed by a short visit to Gibraltar, British Crown Colony before she set out for the U.S. on October 3, 1930.

During his time assigned aboard the *Chester,* Dennison attended the Naval Postgraduate School at Annapolis, Maryland, receiving a Master of Science degree in diesel engineering from Pennsylvania State College.

Following an overhaul at New York Navy Yard during which she was equipped with two catapults amidships, *Chester* stood out of Hampton Roads on July 31, 1932 with planes and ammunition for the West Coast.

She arrived at San Pedro, California, on August 14 and joined in the regular activities of the Pacific fleet. Ensign Richard O'Kane, who would later be awarded the Medal of Honor as the most successful United States submarine officer of World War II, served aboard *Chester* for one year as a junior gun division officer and then as signal officer following his graduation from the Naval Academy in 1934.

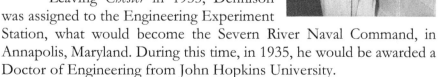

Leaving *Chester* in 1933, Dennison was assigned to the Engineering Experiment Station, what would become the Severn River Naval Command, in Annapolis, Maryland. During this time, in 1935, he would be awarded a Doctor of Engineering from John Hopkins University.

In 1935, Lt. Commander Dennison was given command of the USS *Ortolan* (ASR-5) a minesweeper converted to a submarine rescue ship in September 1929. It was his first command.

The *Ortolan* operated off the California coast with brief exceptions for fleet problems and, in 1936, a four-month tour at Pearl Harbor. In 1937, Dennison transferred aboard the USS *Cuttlefish* (SS-171) as the new captain,

The *Ortolan* returned from the Hawaiian Islands on June 28, 1937, when she sailed for the Panama Canal, Miami, Florida, New York City, and arriving at New London on July 28, where she conducted experimental torpedo firing, sound training, and other operations for the Submarine School.

In 1938, he was assigned as Assistant Naval Inspector of Machinery at the Electric Boat Company, New London Ship and Engine works, Groton, Company involved with the pre-commissioning of submarines, during which time he was promoted to full commander.

On February 4, 1940, Dennison relieved Lt. Commander John D. Shaw to take command of USS *John D. Ford* (DD-228) a Clemson-class destroyer assigned to the Asiatic Fleet, operating out of the Cavite Naval Base, Manila, Philippine Islands.

After the Japanese attack on Pearl Harbor, Hawaii on December 7, 1941, *John D. Ford* readied for action at Cavite as a unit of Destroyer Division 59. Undamaged by the destructive Japanese air raid on Manila Bay on December 10, she sailed southward the same day to patrol the Sulu Sea and Makassar Strait with Task Force 6.

On December 10, Dennison was relieved by Commander Jacob E. Cooper to take a position on the staff of Admiral Thomas C. Hart, Commander-in-Chief, Asiatic Fleet, moving to Australia with Macarthur and the remnants of the Asiatic Fleet. In this assignment he took part in the early war against the Japanese during the campaigns in the Philippines and East Indies. In the winter of 1942 he became Chief of Staff to Commander Allied Naval Forces, East Australia, with similar duty on the staff of Commander Submarines, East Australia.

Detached in August 1942, he became Chief of Staff to Vice Admiral Wilson Brown, Commander Amphibious Force, Pacific Fleet (later 9th Amphibious Force), participating in the seizure and occupation of Attu and Kiska in the Aleutians. Dennison was placed in charge of the planning and execution of assigned missions, handling the various tactical problems with great skill for which he was awarded the Legion of Merit, the citation reading;

"In charge of the planning and execution of an amphibious force mission during the seizure of Attu and Kiska, Territory of Alaska, Captain Dennison handled various tactical problems with high skill. He supervised an attack which enabled our forces to carry out their mission without the loss of ships or personnel."

Late in 1943 he was assigned to the Joint War Plans Committee for the Joint Chiefs of Staff, also serving with distinction as Special Advisor to the Under Secretary of the Navy, with a promotion to the rank of captain. In 1946, following the end of WW II, Dennison was assigned as Assistant Chief of Naval Operations for Politico Military Affairs.

His coordination of foreign policy and naval policy prior to and subsequent to the end of hostilities were performed in such a manner that he was awarded a Gold Star in lieu of a Second Legion of Merit for his outstanding service. On April 2, 1947, Dennison relieved Captain Hill as commanding officer of the USS *Missouri*.

Under Dennison's brief command, *Missouri* operated primarily in the Atlantic sailing north to the Davis Straits and south to the Caribbean on various Atlantic command training exercises.

On August 30, 1947, *Missouri* arrived at Rio de Janeiro for the Inter American Conference for the Maintenance of Hemisphere Peace and Security.

President Harry Truman came aboard on September 2 to celebrate the signing of the Rio Treaty which broadened the Monroe Doctrine, stipulating that an attack on any one of the signatory American States would be considered an attack on all.

Truman and his family boarded *Missouri* on September 7 to return to the United States and disembarked at Norfolk on September

19 after which she went into overhaul in the New York Navy Yard on September 23, 1947 until March 10, 1948. In the interim, Dennison turned command of *Missouri* to Commander John B. Colwell, his executive officer, on January 23, 1948.

On January 23, Dennison was named as naval aide to President Truman, where by all accounts he served more as an advisor than an aide, and he was promoted to rear admiral early in his term. His duties were many and varied. For example, following Defense Secretary James Forrestal's suicide in 1949, Forrestal's estate planned for the publication of his diary.

The diary and related papers of a sensitive nature were placed temporarily in Dennison's custody. He was responsible for providing access to the materials and ensuring that nothing was published that would infringe upon national security.

His term also encompassed the Korean War (June 25, 1950 – July 27, 1953) and Dennison was privy to CIA summaries of events in the Korean conflict, and miscellaneous information concerning the defense of Formosa and other parts of Asia, and Truman often solicited Dennison's views on military matters and he remained in place until the end of the Truman Administration.

In February 1953 Dennison was appointed Commander Cruiser Division 4, operating in the Atlantic, but in January 1954 he was detached for duty as Director of the Strategic Plans Division, Office of the Chief of Naval Operations. There he was given the additional duty as Assistant Chief of Naval Operations (Plans and Policy) from November 14, 1955 until June 1956.

From June 18, 1956 to July 21, 1958, Dennison commanded the 1st Fleet with a promotion to vice-admiral. Upon relinquishing that command, he returned to the Navy Department, where he served as Deputy Chief of Naval Operations (Plans and Policy). On March 31, 1959 he was promoted to the rank of Admiral, as Commander in Chief of Naval Forces, Eastern Atlantic and Mediterranean (CINCNELM).

On February 29, 1960 he was appointed Commander in Chief, Atlantic and US Atlantic Fleet (CINCLANTFOR) and Supreme Allied Commander, Atlantic (SACLANT). These years included the start of civil unrest in the Dominican Republic, an abortive invasion of Cuba by anti-Castro forces at the Bay of Pigs in 1961 and the U.S. naval blockade of Cuba a year later in what came to be known as the Cuban Missile Crisis, also known as the October Crisis of 1962.

Dennison served as commander of the U.S. Unified Command that enforced the blockade and the Joint Chiefs of Staff gave him command of all Army, Navy, Air Force and Marine Corps forces assigned to the action. a force of more than 300,000 men.

From October 16 through November 20, 1962, a confrontation between the United States and the Soviet Union escalated into an international crisis when American deployments of missiles in Italy and Turkey were matched by Soviet deployments of similar ballistic missiles in Cuba. The confrontation is often considered the closest the Cold War came to a full-scale nuclear war.

On Saturday, October 27, after much deliberation between the Soviet Union and President John F. Kennedy's cabinet, Kennedy secretly agreed to remove all missiles set in Turkey and possibly southern Italy, the former on the border of the Soviet Union, in exchange for Soviet Premier Khrushchev removing all missiles in Cuba.

On April 10, 1962, Dennison made the USS *Long Beach* (CGN-160/CGN-9) his flagship. *Long Beach*, a nuclear-powered guided missile cruiser, was the world's first nuclear-powered surface combatant.

Just prior to his retirement, on April 29, 1963, in a Rose Garden ceremony, President Kennedy awarded Admiral Dennison the Distinguished Service Medal. The citation stated:

"for exceptionally meritorious and distinguished service in a position of great responsibility to the Government of the United States from February 1960 to April 1963 as Supreme Allied Commander Atlantic; Commander in Chief, Atlantic; and Commander in Chief, U.S. Atlantic Fleet. Admiral Dennison, as Supreme Allied Commander Atlantic, skillfully directed the highly sensitive aspects of this assignment, and contributed substantially to the high state of readiness and efficiency of the forces of the North Atlantic Treaty Organization. A most significant accomplishment, one with the broadest impact, was his contribution to the successful introduction of the POLARIS submarine into the U.S. Fleet. During the Cuban Crisis of 1962 his leadership and professional skill were demonstrated by his direction of the military forces assigned to his command."

U.S.S. MISSOURI

Left to right: Naval Aide to the President, Captain Tazewell Shepard; President Kennedy; Secretary of the Navy, Fred Korth; unidentified woman; Admiral Dennison; two unidentified men; Chief of Staff of the United States Air Force, General Curtis E. LeMay; Chief of Naval Operations, Admiral George W. Anderson, Jr.; Secretary of Defense, Robert S. McNamara.

Admiral Dennison retired on May 1, 1963 and he was transferred to the Retired List of the US Navy. His awards include Distinguished Service Medal; Legion of Merit with Gold Star; Army Distinguished Unit Emblem (defense of Philippines in December 1941); Navy Unit Commendation Ribbon (USS Pennsylvania, Aleutians Campaign); Order of Naval Merit (Commander) by Government of Brazil; Order of Crown (Cross of Commander) by Belgium; Honorary Officer in the Order of the British Empire, by Great Britain.

Dennison joined the Copley Press in June 1963 and was chairman of the board of the Copley Computer Services for four years before retiring a second time in 1973.

On May 10, 1937, Dennison married Mildred Fenton Mooney Neely, a divorcee with whom he had a daughter, Lee, and son Robert

Lee Jr. He died from a pulmonary embolism at Bethesda Naval Hospital, Maryland on March 14, 1980 at the age of 78. He is buried at Arlington National Cemetery, Arlington, Virginia.

U.S.S. MISSOURI

Commander John B. Colwell

Without a doubt, the shortest tenure in command of the *Missouri* goes to Commander, later Vice Admiral John B. Colwell, who, as executive officer, took command when Captain Dennison departed the ship on January 23, 1948. The ship was in for an overhaul at New York Navy Yard the entire time he was in command. And he was relieved by Captain James H. Thach on February 24, 1948, after only 32 days in command. He would make his mark elsewhere.

John Barr Colwell was born on November 26, 1909 in Pawnee City, Nebraska, the middle of three children born to Clyde George and Mary Bergen Potts Colwell. John, his older sister Mary Elizabeth and younger brother William grew up in a solid middle-class home, their father working as a druggist for Meyer Brothers. Colwell graduated Pawnee City High School in 1926.

Colwell received an appointment to the US Naval Academy from the state of Nebraska, reporting in on June 21, 1927. Known as "Collie", Colwell ranked consistently at the top of his class and in the summer of 1929, he was selected to *"undergo practical instruction in aviation and engineering subjects"*. He graduated 6th in a class of 443 midshipman on June 4, 1931 and was commissioned an ensign in the US Navy.

U.S.S. Missouri

Of the 443 midshipmen in the Class of 1931, 357 were commissioned as line officer, 11 in supply, 24 went to the Marines, 12 graduated but resigned for medical reasons, 36 graduated and voluntarily resigned, 2 were "turned back" to the next lower class due to illness, and one Filipino graduated but was not commissioned.

For five years following his graduation, Colwell served at sea with the Pacific Fleet, serving aboard the battleships USS *Maryland* (BB-46), USS *California* (BB-44) and USS *New York* (BB-34) and the destroyers USS *Rathburne* (DD-113) and USS *Aaron Ward* (DD-132).

Colwell, now a Lieutenant (jg), undertook two years of instruction as the US Navy Postgraduate School, Annapolis, Maryland, where he was promoted to lieutenant on June 30, 1938. He graduated in 1939 with an advanced degree in Ordnance Engineering.

From 1939 until November 1942, Colwell served aboard USS *Idaho* (BB-42) a New Mexico-class battleship, commissioned in March 1919. Initially patrolling the west coast, as tensions began to rise with Japan over its expansionist policies in Asia, the Battle Fleet was transferred from California to Hawaii in summer 1940.

Idaho joined the other ships on July 1. But back in September 1939, World War II had broken out in Europe, spawning the Battle of the Atlantic and in response, President Franklin D. Roosevelt initiated the Neutrality Patrols to protect American shipping.

On May 7, 1941, Admiral Harold Stark, the Chief of Naval Operations, transferred Idaho, her sisters USS *Mississippi* (BB-23) and USS *New Mexico* (BB-40), the aircraft carrier USS *Yorktown* (CV-5), four light cruisers, and two destroyer squadrons to the Atlantic to reinforce the Neutrality Patrols.

Idaho left Hawaii on June 6, bound for Hampton Roads, Virginia to join the neutrality patrols. In September, she was stationed in Hvalfjörður, Iceland, and was there when Japan attacked Pearl Harbor on December 7, 1941.

With the United States now in the war, *Idaho* and *Mississippi* left Iceland on December 9, ordered to rejoin the Pacific Fleet. They docked in Norfolk before passing through the Panama Canal and continuing on to San Francisco, where they arrived on January 31, 1942.

COMMANDER JOHN B. COLWELL

For most of the year, Idaho trained for combat off the coast of California. In October, she sailed to the Puget Sound Navy Yard to receive replacements for her worn out main battery guns. Her original secondary battery of 5-inch/51 cal. guns were removed as these guns were badly needed to arm merchant ships.

Promoted to the rank of temporary commander on November 1, 1942, Colwell left the *Idaho* to take a position as Gunnery Officer on the staff of Admiral William "Bull" Halsey, Commander South Pacific Force.

On January 20, 1944, Colwell relieved Lt. Commander Ellis Hole McDowell at Sydney, Australia to take command of the USS *Converse* (DD-509) a Fletcher-class destroyer commissioned on November 20, 1942, with Commander D. C. E. Hamberger in command. At the time, she was operating in the northern Solomon Islands area as part of Admiral Arleigh Burke's Destroyer Squadron 24 (DESRON24), comprised of seven destroyers and nicknamed "Little Beavers".

Converse rejoined her squadron at Port Purvis on January 30, 1944 conducting bombardments and hunting Japanese shipping through February and March. Between November 1943 and February 1944, *Converse* sank a Japanese cruiser, 9 destroyers, a submarine, several smaller vessels and 30 aircraft, without losing a single ship, actions for which the squadron was awarded a Presidential Unit Citation.

USS CONVERSE (DD-509)

Converse departed from Port Purvis on March 27, 1944 to join Task Force 58 (TF 58) for screening duty during the air strikes on the Palaus from March 30 through April 1, then covered the Hollandia landings through pre-invasion air attacks and bombardment, continuing their fire during the landings on April 22. *Converse* continued screening carrier attacks on Truk, Satawan, and Ponape.

CAPT John Barr Colwell
Photo thanks to Bill Gonyo.

Converse participated in attack preparatory to, and covering, the invasion of Saipan beginning on June 12 as targets throughout the Marianas were hit. While the landings themselves were made on June 15, *Converse*'s task force hit at Japanese bases in the Bonin Islands, and then returned to the Marianas to continue their close support.

When the Japanese fleet challenged the American operations in the Marianas on June 19, she continued her screening through the resulting aerial Battle of the Philippine Sea, a 2-day engagement which resulted in the sinking of three Japanese carriers and the loss to Japan of many aircraft and their irreplaceable pilots. After joining in shore bombardment of Guam and Rota in the final days of June, *Converse* replenished at Eniwetok, and on August 4, sailed for overhaul at Mare Island Naval Shipyard, where Colwell returned command of *Converse* to Lt. Cmdr. McDowell on September 27, 1944.

In September 1944, Colwell reported to the Naval Proving Ground, Dahlgren, Virginia. Dahlgren was involved with new computational devices (computers) because of its ordnance requirements. Ground-breaking early computers were sent to Dahlgren to help with ballistic work and the computer and ordnance work going on attracted a number of brilliant young scientists, some of whom were recruited to help with the ongoing Manhattan Project and the development of the atomic bomb.

These included Dr. Norris E. Bradbury, who later became the Director of the Los Alamos National Laboratory, and "William

Sterling "Deak" Parsons, later the weaponeer on the *Enola Gay*, the aircraft which dropped the Little Boy atomic bomb on Hiroshima, Japan in 1945.

In 1947, Colwell served as the executive officer, and briefly commanding officer of the *Missouri* from January to February 1948. He was promoted to captain on July 1, 1949. After serving on the staff of the Admiral Arthur W. Radford, Commander-in-Chief Pacific Fleet (CINCPACFLT), Colwell served in the Bureau of Ordnance, responsible for the procurement, storage, and deployment of all naval weapons from 1951-53, followed by duty as an aide and administrative assistant to William Chapman Foster, the Deputy Secretary of Defense, in Washington DC.

In May 1954, Colwell took command of the Cimarron-class fleet oiler USS *Elokomin* (AO-55). Based out of Norfolk, Virginia, she operated mainly along the east coast and on fleet exercises.

After being relieved by Captain Edward Ellis Shelby in October 1955, Colwell reported as the Deputy Director Fleet Ballistic Missile Project at Cape Canaveral, Florida.

For his work in developing the Polaris Missile, Colwell was awarded the Legion of Merit, the citation stating:

"he succeeded in forming a group of high-caliber personnel, well versed in all aspects of missile development. The outstanding progress achieved by the Navy in the field of ballistic missiles can be attributed in large measure to his ability to mold a coordinated team of individuals and groups from government, industry, and universities under the direction of the Special Projects Office, for the purpose of developing a Fleet Ballistic Missile system."

In May 1958, Colwell left the missile project and reported to Philadelphia to take command of the newly commissioned USS *Galveston* (CLG-93), a Cleveland-class light cruiser that was converted into a Galveston-class guided missile cruiser, the US Navy's first.

Galveston departed Philadelphia on June 30, 1958 for sea trials in the Virginia Capes off of Norfolk, Virginia that included "highly successful" tests of her new *Talos* missile and tracking gear. The *Talos* was a supersonic surface-to-air missile that was 38 ft long, weighed nearly 3,000 pounds, and was powered by a novel 20,053 lbf ramjet engine, plus a solid-fuel rocket booster. With a range of over 65 miles for early variants, and over 100 for later ones, it could reach speeds of up to Mach 4 and was designed to destroy enemy aircraft at high altitudes using either a conventional or atomic warhead.

Galveston finished out 1958 with operations in the Norfolk area, and on November 18, 1958, Colwell turned command over to Captain David D. Scott. In 1959, he was promoted to rear admiral, followed by a number of assignments in Washington DC including as a member of General Planning Group in the Office of the Chief of Naval Operations (CNO), Senior Naval Assistant to the Director of Defense Research and Engineering, Office of the Secretary of Defense and Director of the Long-Range Objectives Group in the Office of the CNO.

On January 17, 1964, Colwell, now a vice-admiral, was named Commander Amphibious Force, US Pacific Fleet while the United States was heavily involved in the conflict in Vietnam.

On May 10, 1965, Admiral Colwell was named Deputy Chief of Naval Operations for Fleet Operations and Readiness and his direction of naval assets in Vietnam resulted in the award of the Navy Distinguished Service Medal for: "*His singularly distinctive accomplishments and his dedicated contributions in the service of his country.*"

Colwell retired from the Navy as a vice-admiral in July 1969 after 42 years of service and he retired to Arlington County, Virginia and Naples, Florida before settling in Takoma Park, Maryland, working as a consultant to various defense corporations.

Colwell married Grace Arent in 1939 and had three sons and a daughter. Colwell died at home from respiratory failure on February 5, 2008, at the age of 98. He and his wife, who died in 1993, are buried together in the Naval Academy Cemetery, Annapolis, Maryland.

Captain John Smith Thach

Unlike the majority of *Missouri*'s skippers, Captain Thach's expertise would be naval aviation in which he would become both a pioneer and a legend. He developed both the Thach Weave, a combat flight formation developed to counter enemy fighters of superior performance, and the big blue blanket, an aerial defense against kamikaze attacks, methods he would himself prove effective in aerial combat in WW II and Korea.

Photo # K-13945   LCdr. John S. Thach, circa 1942-43

John Smith Thach was born in Pine Bluff, Jefferson County, Arkansas on April 19, 1905 to James Harmon Thach and Jo Bocage Smith Thatch, both of whom were schoolteachers. His older brother, James Harmon "Jimmie" Thach would also have a distinguished naval career.

After graduating Fordyce High School, Thatch followed his older brother James (USNA Class of 1923) into the US Naval Academy being appointed from the state of Arkansas on July 9, 1923. He became known as "Little Jimmie" as his brother James was given the nickname "Jimmie".

Thach played football for the academy, but because of his thin frame, he was placed on the practice team, opposing the varsity team in practice.

Two dislocated shoulders ended his dreams of gridiron glory, and impacted his studies, graduating 489 in a class of 579 on June 2, 1927 with a commission as ensign in the US Navy. He and 262 others in his class were retained for aviation instruction in the summer of 1927.

Despite his low academic standing, Thach was well regarded by his classmates. As he was remembered in the Academy's 1927 Lucky Bag, "Jack has every characteristic of a true gentleman of the old South, and these, combined with his high ideals are bound to gain a career of success and happiness."

On August 26, 1927 Ensign Thach's first ship assignment was aboard the battleship USS *Mississippi* (BB-41) where he served until May 1928, operating in the Pacific. On June 7, 1928 Thach was assigned to the staff of Vice Admiral Louis McCoy Nulton, the Commander-in-Chief of the Battle Fleet (Atlantic) aboard battleship USS *California* (BB-44).

On March 28, 1929, Thach was under instruction at Naval Air Station Pensacola, Florida. On January 4, 1930, Ensign Thach was designated a Naval Aviator and awarded his wings of gold.

On March 8, 1930 Lt.(jg) Thach was assigned to WW I era minelayer USS *Aroostook* (CM-3) which during the spring of 1919 had been refitted as an "aircraft tender" and he was assigned as engineering officer for Utility Squadron 1B (VJ-1B) but in June, he transferred aboard aircraft carrier USS *Saratoga* (CV-3), assigned to Fighter Squadron 1B (VF-1B)

From June 1930 through June 1932, Thach was a member of "Fighting One", also known as the "High Hats" for their logo, a tuxedo-style high hat. Thach and his squadron performed stunt work for Clark Gable's 1931 movie *Hell Divers*. This squadron was well known for demonstrating formation flying skill.

Saratoga operated in the Pacific, developing and refining carrier tactics in a series of annual exercises and Thach proved himself a capable pilot, repeatedly shooting top scores in every type of combat aircraft he flew, becoming recognized as one of the Navy's aerial gunnery experts.

In December 1931, Thach married Dora Madalyn Jones with whom they had two sons John Smith Thach Jr. and William Leland Thach.

On July 1, 1932 Thach was assigned to Naval Air Station, Norfolk Virginia, as a test pilot. He set endurance records during this period with experimental aircraft. On June 29, 1934, Thach, now a Lieutenant, was assigned to Patrol Squadron 9-F (VP-9F) aboard sea plane tender USS *Wright* (AV-1). While in this assignment he was ordered back to NAS Norfolk for a special assignment.

He piloted an experimental aircraft, a Hall XP2H four engine biplane flying boat seaplane, setting a record flying from Norfolk, Virginia, to Panama in less than twenty-six hours. He left VP-9 in June 1936, to report to Scouting Squadron 6-B (VS-6B) on July 1, 1936.

Embarked aboard the light cruiser USS *Cincinnati* (CL-6) an Omaha-class light cruiser, originally classified as a scout cruiser commissioned January 1, 1924, the squadron flew Curtiss SOC-1 *Seagulls*.

The *Seagull* was a single-engine scout observation seaplane, designed by Curtiss-Wright for the United States Navy. The aircraft served on battleships and cruisers in a seaplane configuration, being launched by catapult and recovered from a sea landing. The wings folded back against the fuselage for storage aboard ship.

Cincinnati operated in the Pacific as part of the Battle Force and it was during this assignment that Thach qualified as officer of the deck, remaining aboard until June 20, 1937 when he was assigned to Patrol Squadron Five (VP-5F) "Mad Foxes" at Fleet Air Base Coco Solo, Canal Zone.

In October 1937, VP-5F was re-designated VP-5 when Navy patrol squadrons were reorganized under the command of Patrol Wings. VPs 5, 2 and 3 came under Patrol Wing-3, NAS Coco Solo.

On May 14, 1938, VP-5 departed Coco Solo for NAS Norfolk, where the squadron turned in their P2Y-2 seaplanes. On May 18, the squadron arrived at NAS San Diego, California, to receive replacement PBY-3 Catalina aircraft and transition training in the new seaplanes.

The squadron returned to NAS Coco Solo on September 14, 1938. He remained with the squadron until May 1939. On June 30, 1939, Thach was assigned as gunnery officer and later executive officer, then Commanding Officer of Fighting Squadron Three (VF-3) with the insignia of "Felix the Cat". The squadron was equipped with the Brewster F2A *Buffalos*, one of the first U.S. monoplanes equipped with an arrestor-hook and other modifications for use on aircraft carriers and was the U.S. Navy's first monoplane fighter aircraft.

As the commander of Fighting Three squadron, Lt. Commander Thach knew from access to intelligence reports, specifically a Fleet Air Tactical Unit Intelligence Bulletin dated September 22, 1941, that his unit was equipped with aircraft that could not match the performance standard set by Japanese fighter airplanes, and like most military leaders of the time, he believed that the question of war with Japan was a matter of "when", not "if".

Thach's VF-3 squad transitioned to the Grumman F4F *Wildcat,* a big improvement over the *Buffalo* but even with a top speed of 318 mph, the *Wildcat* was still outperformed by the faster (331 mph), more maneuverable, faster climbing and longer-ranged Mitsubishi A6M *Zero.*

Thach believed that these advantages could be overcome with superior marksmanship as well as tactics.

As the Commander of VF-3, he mentored new pilots, including a new ensign fresh from flight training, Edward O'Hare who he selected as his wingman.

Towards the end of 1940, during the Naval Fleet Gunnery Competition, 8 of the 16 pilots of VF-3 qualified for the Gunnery "E" for Excellence award, and Thach was recognized with a letter of commendation for *"exceptional skill and technique in aerial gunnery and bombing; efficient and meticulous operation of a squadron gunnery department; marked ability to train other pilots in fighting plane tactics and gunnery."*

As for tactics, he began to devise tactics meant to give the slower-turning Wildcat fighters a chance against the move maneuverable *Zero*'s in combat. While based in San Diego, he spent his time working on different tactics that could overcome the Zero's maneuverability and then he would test them in flight the following day.

At the time, the standard practice was a six-plane division broken into two three-plane sections which had been used for years, but after the beginning of the war in Europe, in 1939, some began to question its efficacy. A July 29, 1940 confidential memo to Rear Admiral William F. Halsey Jr. written by Lt. Commander Miles Browning, the Officer in Charge, Fleet Tactical Unit contributed to the rejection. Browning championed the continuing use of the six-plane VF unit, suggesting it contributed in part to British success in aerial battles early in the Battle of Britain.

However, in the summer of 1941, Halsey reversed his decision and directed that each eighteen-plane fighter squadron he comprised of three six plane divisions with each division organized into three two plane sections. Freed from the three-plane restriction in July 1941, Thach was able to concentrate on how a two-plane section could best counter the Zero.

Working at night with matchsticks on the table, he eventually came up with what he called "Beam Defense Position", but it soon became known as the "Thach Weave". The theory behind the beam attack was predicated on a two-plane formation.

The "Thach Weave" was executed either by two fighter aircraft side-by-side or by two pairs of fighters flying together, at a distance of approximately the tactical turning radius of the *Wildcat*. When an enemy aircraft chose one fighter as his target, (the "bait" fighter with his wingman being the "hook"), the two wingmen would turn in towards each other. After crossing paths, and once their separation was great enough, they would then repeat the exercise, again turning in towards each other, bringing the enemy plane into the hook's sights. If correctly executed, assuming the bait was taken and followed, it left little chance of escape to even the most maneuverable foe.

Two squadrons, VF-2 and VF-5 were directed to test the two-plane section. Enthusiastic statements favoring the two-plane section were reported by both squadrons, but the real test would come in actual aerial combat. The wait wasn't a long one, as the Japanese attacked Pearl Harbor on December 7, 1941. The first test came on February 20, 1942.

On December 5, 1941, and Task Force 12 (TF-12) centered around aircraft carrier USS *Lexington* (CV-2) along with three heavy cruisers and five destroyers departed Pearl Harbor to ferry 18 U.S. Marine Corps Vought SB2U Vindicator dive bombers of VMSB-231 to reinforce the base at Midway Island. Also embarked were 68 of her own aircraft (21 Buffalos, 32 Douglas SBD Dauntless dive bombers, and 15 Douglas TBD Devastator torpedo bombers), and were at sea when the Japanese attacked.

The ferry mission was canceled, and TF-12 was ordered to search for the Japanese ships while rendezvousing with Vice Admiral Wilson Brown's ships 100 miles west of Niihau Island. On February 12, 1942, the 18 Grumman F4F *Wildcats* of VF-3, redeployed from the torpedoed USS Saratoga, embarked on *Lexington*, and replaced VF-2 to allow the latter unit to convert from *Buffalos* to the *Wildcat*.

Now, on February 20, *Lexington* intruded into Japanese-held waters north of New Ireland in the Bismarck Archipelago. In the afternoon, the carrier came under attack by several flights of enemy Mitsubishi G4M *"Betty"* bombers.

Lexington's VF-3 *Wildcats*, were launched in defense and an air battle ensued. Another flight of nine Bettys approached from the undefended side, and Lt. (jg) "Butch" O'Hare, now a section leader, and his wingman were the first fighter pilots available to intercept.

At about 5pm, O'Hare arrived over the nine incoming bombers and attacked. His wingman's guns failed, so O'Hare fought on alone. In the air battle, he is credited with having shot down five of the Japanese bombers and damaging a sixth, becoming an ace in one action.

For his actions, Butch O'Hare was promoted to Lieutenant Commander and on April 21, 1942, FDR presented O'Hare the Medal of Honor as Secretary of the Navy Frank Knox, Admiral Ernest King and his wife Rita looked on. O'Hare, commanding Air Group 6 from

USS *Enterprise* (CV-6), was killed in action on the night of November 27, 1944, when his Grumman *Hellcat* was shot down by a Mitsubishi

G4M bomber. He was posthumously awarded the Navy Cross for his actions during Operation *Galvanic*, November 26, 1943.

Thach was awarded the Navy Cross for his actions, the citation reading:

"for extraordinary heroism in operations against the enemy while serving as Pilot of a carrier-based Navy Fighter Plane and Commanding Officer of Fighting Squadron THREE (VF3), attached to the U.S.S. LEXINGTON (CV-2), when on 20 February 1942, in enemy waters, he led his Squadron in repeated attacks against two nine-plane formations of Japanese twin-engine heavy bombers which resulted in the destruction of sixteen of the eighteen enemy aircraft engaged. Through his courage and skill, he shot down one enemy bomber, and with the assistance of his teammates, shot down a second bomber."

Another test, this time with a larger group of aircraft, occurred during the Battle of the Coral Sea, May 4-8, 1942, the first action in which aircraft carriers engaged each other and the first in which the opposing ships neither sighted nor fired directly upon one another.

Later, at the Battle of Midway, June 3-7, 1942, the widespread employment of the maneuver by planes flying from the USS *Yorktown* (CV-5), when Thach led a six-plane sortie from VF-3, escorting twelve Douglas TBD *Devastators* of VT-3 led by Lieutenant Commander Lance Massey, when they discovered the main Japanese carrier fleet. They were immediately attacked by 15 to 20 Japanese fighters. Thach decided to use his namesake maneuver and managed to shoot down three *Zeros* and a wingman accounted for another, at the cost of one Grumman F4F *Wildcat*.

Thach was awarded a second Navy Cross:

"for action against enemy Japanese forces during the "Air Battle of Midway," on 4 June 1942. Pursuing the bold and fearless tactics of a great fighter and a skillful airman, Lieutenant Commander Thach led a division of his squadron on a mission providing protection for our own attacking torpedo squadron.

Facing intense anti-aircraft fire, the squadron under his efficient command, attacked an overwhelming number of Japanese fighters, shooting down three of them. Again, in the afternoon, he led a determined and effective attack against enemy torpedo planes which were attacking his carrier, shooting down one of them in this engagement."

Deemed too valuable to risk in combat, in July 1942 Thach was assigned on the staff of the Chief of Naval Air Operational Training at Naval Air Station (NAS), Jacksonville, Florida, where he was promoted to commander, instructing other pilots in combat tactics, and creating training films. Although not happy with the assignment, it made sense.

The US Navy pulled its best combat pilots out of action to train newer pilots, while the Japanese kept their best pilots in combat. As the war progressed, the Japanese Navy lost their experienced pilots due to attrition and lacked well-trained replacements, while the United States was able to improve the general fighting ability of their own pilots.

In June 1944, after requesting a combat assignment, Thach was assigned as Operations Officer to Vice Admiral John S. McCain's fast carrier Task Group 38.1 (TG-38.1). During this time, he was awarded the Silver Star Medal for the period 13 through 15 October 1944, off Formosa.

As the citation states:

"While the Task Group was covering the withdrawal of two crippled cruisers against repeated and persistent enemy air attacks, his skillful handling of our air forces, effective strategy and unerring judgment forced the enemy to break off his attacks, and in a large measure contributed to the salvaging of the crippled ships."

He was also awarded the Legion of Merit with Combat "V" (Valor) for:

"exceptional ingenuity as a tactician and utilization of previously unexploited aircraft potentialities resulted in devastating damage to enemy aircraft, shipping, and ground installations. The successful accomplishment of the missions under his direction made possible the re-capture of vastly important territories in the war of the Pacific."

Toward the end of the war, in response to devastating suicidal Kamikaze attacks, Thach developed the "Big Blue Blanket" defense wherein there was a continuous patrol by carrier-based aircraft over enemy airfields, preventing take-offs and destroying them on the ground. Awarded a Bronze Star Medal, he was credited with designing a *"successful Task Force fighter defense against Japanese kamikaze attack."*

In the last two months of the war not one carrier was hit. On September 2, 1945, newly promoted Captain Thatch was present on the deck of the USS *Missouri,* by invitation of Admiral Halsey, to witness the Japanese surrender. From September 1945 to April 1950, Captain Thach was back on the staff of the Chief of Naval Air Training at Naval Air Station Pensacola, teaching the next generation of naval aviators.

On June 15, 1950, Thach took command of the USS *Sicily* (CVE-118) a Commencement-class escort aircraft carrier commissioned on February 27, 1946. On April 3, 1950, *Sicily* departed Norfolk, sailing through the Panama Canal to her new assignment to San Diego as part of the Pacific Fleet, where Thach came aboard. Five months later, on June 25, the United States was again at war, this time in Korea.

The *Sicily* was scheduled for Anti-submarine warfare (ASW) exercises but on July 2, Thach received orders to prepare to sail for the Far East and two-days later, on July 4, *Sicily* departed for the first of what would be three deployments to Korea.

Sicily served as the flagship for Rear Admiral Richard W. Ruble's Escort Carrier Task Group (TG 96.8). Ruble had been awarded a Silver Star as navigator of the carrier Enterprise (CV-6) during the Doolittle Raid and the battles of Midway, Eastern Solomons, and Santa Cruz in World War II.

On August 3, 1950 eight F4U-4B *Corsairs* of Marine Attack Squadron (VMF-214) executed a raid against enemy installations near Inchon. After the *Corsairs* delivered their incendiary bombs and rockets, they followed up with a series of strafing run. It was the first US airstrike in support of ground forces during the Korean War.

The VMF-214 *"Black Sheep"* had a colorful history and a legendary commander, Colonel Gregory "Pappy" Boyington, who was awarded the Medal of Honor posthumously during WW II, and then a second time by President Truman after returning the US following being released from a Japanese POW camp.

Sicily supported operations at Pohang, the landing at Inchon, the advance on Seoul and covered the withdrawals from the Chosin Reservoir and Hungham, before returning to San Diego on February 5, 1951.

Thach took *Sicily* on a second deployment into Korean waters, departing San Diego on May 13, and operated off both the east and west coast of Korea until October 12, 1951, but Thach turned command over to Captain William Alton Schoech on August 11, 1951.

From August through December 1951, Thach served as Chief of Staff to Commander Carrier Division 7 (COMCARDIV7) then was assigned as an aide to the Assistant Secretary of the Navy for Air until May 1953.

On May 22, Thach relieved Captain George W. Anderson to take command of the USS *Franklin D. Roosevelt* (CVA-42) one of three Midway-class aircraft carriers, commissioned on October 27, 1945.

The *Roosevelt* participated in NATO exercises in the North Atlantic and Mediterranean until she was temporarily decommissioned at the Puget Sound Naval Shipyard for a refit on April 23, 1954, the same day Thach transferred command to Captain John Taylor Hayward.

Photo # NH 96872 R.Adm. John S. Thach, 1957

It was his last command of a US warship at sea.

From April 1954 until August 1955, Thach was Commander- Naval Air Bases, 6th Naval District at Jacksonville, Florida, with promotion to rear admiral in November 1955, then he served as the Senior Naval Member of the Military Studies and Liaison Division of the Weapons Evaluation Group at the Pentagon in Washington DC until October 1957.

In November of 1957, Thach took command of Carrier Division 16 (CARDIV16) and from 1958-59, Thach pioneered new tactics in anti-submarine warfare in command of the Anti-submarine Development Unit, "Task Group Alpha" with the aircraft Carrier USS *Valley Forge* (CV-45) serving as his flagship.

He appeared on the cover of TIME Magazine on September 1, 1958, and the Navy established the Admiral Thach Award, an annual given to the top ASW squadron.

In January 1960, Thach was promoted to vice admiral, serving as Deputy Chief of Naval Operations for Air at the Pentagon, where he presided over the development of the A-7 *Corsair* II as well as other aircraft programs.

In March 1965, Thach was promoted to full admiral and was appointed Commander-in-Chief of U.S. Naval Forces in Europe where he served until his retirement in May 1967, after more than 40 years naval service.

Admiral Thach retired to Coronado, California where he died on April 15, 1981, 4 days before his 76th birthday and was buried at the Fort Rosecrans National Cemetery, San Diego. On March 17, 1983, the USS *Thatch* (FFG-43), an Oliver Hazard Perry-class guided missile frigate, was named in his honor.

U.S.S. Missouri

Captain Harold P. Smith

Harold P. Smith would have as varied and distinguished a naval career as any man who ever commanded the *Missouri*. A Naval Academy graduate, he would serve aboard battleships and cruisers, command a destroyer in combat, for which he would be awarded the Navy Cross and command America's most celebrated and revered warship the *Missouri*, one of only three men to command her twice. He would finish his 40-year career with the 4-stars of a full admiral.

Harold Page Smith was born on February 17, 1904 in the small hamlet of Grand Bay, Alabama, located in the southwestern corner of Mobile County on the border with Mississippi. He was the middle of three children born to Harvey Samuel Smith and Elizabeth Zilpha (Warren) Smith. He, his older sister Mildred and younger brother Leighton grew up in the sparsely populated rural community.

Appointed to the US Naval Academy from Alabama, Smith reported in on June 29, 1920 at the age of 16 years, 4 months. Known as "Smitty" and remembered as being a bit of a "ladies' man" in the Lucky Bag, Smith wrested and ran track, and graduated 226 out of 545 in June 1924 with a commission as ensign.

His first assignment was to the New Mexico-Class battleship USS *Idaho* (BB-42). Commissioned in March 1919, *Idaho* was assigned to the Battle Fleet (Pacific) and in 1925 conducted fleet exercises in Hawaii and made port visits to Samoa, Australia and New Zealand.

U.S.S. MISSOURI

In 1925, Smith reported aboard the USS *Procyon* (AG-11), an Antares-Class cargo ship. *Procyon* served as the Flagship of Rear Admiral S.E.W. Kittelle, Commander Fleet Base Force – US Battle Fleet where he was promoted to lieutenant (jg) before leaving the ship in 1928.

From 1928-29, Smith served as a division officer aboard the USS *Arizona* (BB-39) a Pennsylvania-Class battleship commissioned October 17, 1916 and operating in the Pacific. In 1929, Smith transferred to the USS *Nevada* (BB-36) the lead ship of the Nevada--Class battleship, commissioned on March 11, 1916 and a WW I veteran. After being modernized at the Norfolk Naval Shipyard in Virginia (August 1927 through January 1930) *Nevada* operated off the Pacific coast conducting the usual exercises and inspections.

Following a two-year assignment as an Instructor in the Modern Language Department at the Naval Academy (1932-33), where he was promoted to full lieutenant, Smith served as gunnery officer aboard the destroyer USS *Farragut* (DD-348) from 1934 through 1937.

Homeported at Norfolk, Virginia, she embarked from Jacksonville, Florida on March 26, 1935, with President Franklin D. Roosevelt aboard and the next day carried him to a rendezvous with a private yacht. *Farragut* escorted the President's yacht on a cruise to the Bahamas. On April 7, FDR again embarked on her for passage back to Jacksonville, where he left the ship on April 8.

Farragut sailed for San Diego, California, arriving there on April 19, 1935 to join the Pacific fleet as flagship of Destroyer Squadron 20 (DESRON20). *Farragut* operated conducting fleet maneuvers on the west coast, training operations in the Hawaiian Islands, and cruises during the summer to train men of the Naval Reserve in Alaskan waters. He left Farragut in 1937.

Promoted to lieutenant-commander on April 1, 1939, Smith took command of the Clemson-Class destroyer USS *Stewart* (DD-224) on May 18, 1940. A WW I era four-stacker commissioned September 15, 1920, she entered the Cavite Navy Yard in the Philippines for overhaul on April 5, 1940. Upon leaving the yard on June 1, *Stewart* acted as plane guard vessel for seaplanes flying between Guam and the Philippines and then made a tour of Chinese Yellow Sea ports from July 7 to September 23, 1940.

During 1941, *Stewart* remained in the Philippines as tensions between the United States and Japan worsened and, on November 27, she was ordered, along with the other major surface combatants of the Asiatic Fleet, to the Dutch East Indies.

Stewart was at Tarakan Roads, Borneo, with other American and Dutch ships, when news of the Japanese attack reached them on December 8. During the final weeks of 1941, she escorted naval auxiliaries from the Philippines to Port Darwin, Australia.

On January 9, 1942 *Stewart* was one of five destroyers in an escort composed of the light cruisers USS *Boise* (CL-47) and USS *Marblehead* (CL-12), with Clemson-class destroyers USS *Bulmer* (DD-222), USS *Pope* (DD-225), USS *Parrott* (DD-218), and USS *Barker* (DD-213) departing from Darwin to Surabaya escorting the transport *Bloemfontein*.

The *Bloemfontein*, part of the Pensacola Convoy, had left Brisbane on December 30, 1941 with Army reinforcements composed of the 26th Field Artillery Brigade and Headquarters Battery, the 1st Battalion, 131st Field Artillery and supplies destined for Java.

On January 20, *Stewart* and *Barker* was ordered to Ratai Bay, Sumatra to escort troop convoy MS-2 that arrived that day from Ceylon. The convoy consisted of the large British liner *Aquitania* with 3,500 Australian troops reinforcements for Singapore, escorted by the Australian cruiser HMAS *Canberra*, and three warships of the Royal Netherland Navy, the Dutch light cruiser HNLMS *Java* and the destroyers HNLMS *Evertsen* and HNLMS *Van Nes*.

Since the Japanese held air supremacy over Singapore and its approaches, it was decided to transfer the troops to smaller vessels. The troops were transferred to Dutch KPM steamers *Both, Reael, Reynst, Van Der Lijn, Van Swoll, Sloet, Van De Belle, Taishan* and a British ship.

Cover during the transfer was provided by the *Canberra*, light cruiser HMS *Dragon*, destroyers *Stewart, Barker*, HMAS *Vampire*, HMS *Express, Van Nes* and patrol boats USS *Isabel* and HNLMS *Soemba*.

On January 21, the convoy, now called MS-2A, departed Ratai Bay for Singapore. As the convoy neared the north end of the Sunda

Strait, all of the escorts were detached except *Java* and *Thanet* and the convoy arrived safely at Singapore on January 24.

On January 30, *Stewart* joined Marblehead and on February 4, moved to intercept a Japanese convoy at the south entrance to the Macassar Strait. In the ensuing Battle of Makassar Strait, *Marblehead* was badly-damaged when a wave of seven bombers released bombs at *Marblehead*. Two were direct hits and a third, a near miss close aboard the port bow, caused severe underwater damage and Stewart escorted her back to the base at Tjilatjap, Java.

On February 14, Stewart joined Dutch Admiral Karel Doorman's striking force under the ABDA (American-British-Dutch-Australian) Command for an attack on Japanese forces advancing along the northern coast of Sumatra.

As the convoy approached, *Stewart* had to back her engines to avoid a Dutch destroyer ahead of her which had run aground on a reef in Stolze Strait, and, on the following day, February 15, she survived numerous air attacks in the Bangka Strait. Although they damaged no Allied ships, the air attacks convinced Doorman that any further advance without air cover would be reckless, and the Allied force retired. On February 16, *Stewart* returned to Sumatra to refuel.

Doorman's forces were scattered when the Japanese landed on Bali on February 19, it could not be ignored because it would give the Japanese an airbase within range of the ABDA naval base at Surabaya. With no time to concentrate his ships, Doorman deployed his ships against the enemy piecemeal, in three groups on the night of 19 and 20 February in the Battle of Badung Strait.

In the engagement, four Japanese destroyers defeated an Allied force that outnumbered and outgunned them, driving off the much larger Allied force, sinking the destroyer HNLMS *Piet Hein*, damaging the destroyer *Stewart* and severely damaging the cruiser HLNMS *Tromp*. Meanwhile, the Japanese had sustained little damage themselves, and had protected their transport ships.

For his actions, Smith was awarded the Navy Cross, the citation reading:

"as Commanding Officer of the Destroyer U.S.S. STEWART (DD-224), in action against a greatly superior Japanese Naval force in the Badoeng

Strait, off the Island of Bali, Netherlands East Indies, on the night of 19 - 20 February 1942. Although under heavy fire from the enemy, Lieutenant Commander Smith pressed home the attack which resulted in severe damage to the enemy, while receiving minor damage to his own ship and only one casualty to his personnel."

On February 22, *Stewart,* as the most severely damaged ship, was the first to enter the 15,500-ton floating drydock at Surabaya for repairs. However, she was inadequately supported in the dock, and as the dock rose, the ship fell off the keel blocks onto her side in 12 feet water, bending her propeller shafts and causing further hull damage.

Under enemy air attack and in danger of falling to the enemy, the ship could not be repaired. Responsibility for the destruction of the ship was left with the naval authorities ashore, and *Stewart*'s last crew members departed the embattled port on the afternoon of February 22.

Subsequently, demolition charges were set off within the ship, a Japanese bomb exploded amidships further damaging her, and before the port was evacuated on March 2, the drydock containing her was scuttled before the Japanese arrived.

In February 1943, after almost a year under water, Stewart was raised by the Japanese and commissioned into the Imperial Japanese Navy on September 20, 1943 as Patrol Boat No. 102, under the command of Lt. Mizutani Tamotsu. She was armed with two 3-inch guns and operated with the Japanese Southwest Area Fleet on escort duty until she was bombed and damaged by United States Army aircraft at Mokpo, Korea on April 28, 1945. She was transferred to the control of the Kure Navy District, and in August 1945, was found by American occupation forces laid up in Hiro Bay near Kure.

Smith returned to the United States to a hero's welcome and was assigned to a War Bonds tour of ten British and five Americans decorated for valor. On June 7, 1942, after being greeted by New York Mayor Fiorello La Guardia, they were given a parade through Times Square to a crowd of 40,000, lunch at the Astor Hotel, they appeared at a War Bond Rally at Madison Square Garden to a crowd of 15,000.

Besides Smith, the other four Americans honored were Ensign Donald F. Mason, awarded a Distinguished Flying Cross and Silver

Star who sent the message: "Sighted sub, sank same." Lt. Elliott Vandevanter Jr. awarded the D.F.C. for gallantry at the request of Gen. MacArthur, Lt. William C. Carrithers, cited for skill as a navigator on a raid on the Japanese and Lt. George S. "Welch, awarded a Distinguished Service Cross for shooting down four Japanese planes at Pearl Harbor.

Following the War Bond Tour, Smith was assigned to the War Plans Section on the staff of the Admiral Royal E. Ingersoll, Commander US Atlantic Fleet until early 1944 when he appointed Commander Destroyer Squadron 4 (DESRON 4) for which he was twice awarded the Legion of Merit for his skillful and gallant action while leading successful combat operations from his flagship, USS *Selfridge* (DD-357) commanding Destroyer Divisions 7 and 8.

As his Legion of Merit documents "Captain Harold Page Smith, United States Navy, was awarded the Legion of Merit for "exceptionally meritorious conduct in the performance of outstanding services to the Government of the United States as Commander Destroyer Squadron FOUR, at Wake, Marcus, Volcano and Bonin Islands, from 4 September 1944 to 5 January 1945."

On February 5, 1949, Smith relieved Captain James Thach as commanding officer of the *Missouri* and she participated in Atlantic command exercises from New England to the Caribbean, alternated with two midshipman summer training cruises. She went into the Norfolk Naval Shipyard on September 23, 1949 for an overhaul and Smith turned over command to Captain William D. Brown on December 10, 1949.

Despite several vessels of various types being decommissioned, President Truman refused to allow *Missouri* to be decommissioned. Against the advice of Secretary of Defense Louis Johnson, Secretary of the Navy John L. Sullivan, and Chief of Naval Operations Louis E. Denfeld, Truman ordered *Missouri* to be maintained with the active fleet partly because of his fondness for the battleship.

Then the only U.S. battleship in commission, *Missouri* was proceeding seaward on a training mission from Hampton Roads early on January 17, 1950 when she ran aground, leading to a Court Martial for Brown and two other officers, and command was briefly turned over to the executive officer, Commander George E. Peckham until Smith returned to take command on February 7, 1950.

On April 19, 1950, Smith turned over command to Captain Irving T. Duke. After a short period as Chief of Staff to Rear Admiral Felix L. Johnson, the Commander Destroyer Force – Atlantic Fleet (COMDESFORLANT), Smith was appointed Deputy Chief of Information in the Office of the Chief of Naval Operations, then from 1951-1953, he worked in the Office of the Secretary of Defense.

Photo # 80-G-414591 USS Missouri change of command, April 1950

From 1955-56, Smith, newly promoted to rear admiral, worked in the Office of Comptroller of the Navy where he worked as an aide to Asst. Secretary of the Navy William B. Franke, dealing with the budget and fiscal matters.

On January 28, 1958, Smith was named Chief of Naval Personnel and Chief of the Bureau of Naval Personnel and was promoted to Vice Admiral. As part of his duties, he was placed in charge of arranging the funerals for Fleet Admiral William D. Leahy, the senior-most United States military officer on active duty during World War II who died July 20, 1959, and Fleet Admiral William F. "Bull Halsey, who died August 16, 1959. As two of only four 5-star admirals in history, their lying in state at the National Cathedral and burial at Arlington National Cemetery with full military honors required extensive preparations and logistics.

Also, while Chief of Personnel, Smith was requested by Fleet Admiral Chester Nimitz to intervene on his behalf with Congressman Carl Vinson, Chairman of the House Naval Affairs Committee, later to become the House Armed Services Committee, regarding promoting Admiral Raymond A. Spruance to the rank of Fleet Admiral.

Towards the end of World War II, Congress had authorized four Naval four-star officers to be promoted to the 5-star rank of Fleet Admiral. Admirals Leahy, Nimitz, and Ernest King were selected, but there was a debate between Halsey and Spruance for the fourth slot.

A staunch supporter of Admiral Halsey, Vinson blocked Spruance's nomination several times, although others thought Spruance more deserving to ensure that Halsey got the fourth billet. Although Smith met with Vinson and conveyed Nimitz's request, he was unable to persuade him to agreeing to the late promotion, Vinson responding *"We should leave that exalted rank for a major war...You tell Admiral Nimitz with my deepest respect and my best hopes, and so on, that we're going to leave it just like it is."*

On February 1, 1960, Smith was promoted to full admiral and relieved Admiral Robert Dennison as Commander in Chief US Naval Forces Europe (CINCUSNAVEUR) with the concurrent duty as Commander in Chief Eastern Atlantic and Mediterranean (CINCNELM).

Three years later, on April 30, 1963 Smith again relieved Admiral Dennison, this time as Supreme Allied Commander Atlantic (SACLANT) Commander-in-Chief, Atlantic Command (CINCLANT); and Commander-in-Chief, U.S. Atlantic Fleet (CINCLANTFLT).

He served in those commands until he was relieved by Admiral Thomas Moorer upon Smith's retirement from the Navy on May 1, 1965.

On May 4, 1965, in a ceremony in the White House Rose Garden, President Lyndon Baines Johnson presented Admiral Smith with the Distinguished Service Medal. In his remarks, Johnson stated:

"In the Pacific and in the Atlantic during World War II, Admiral Smith established a memorable record of courage and valor and leadership. Following the war, he held many important commands, both ashore and at sea. None was more vital than the one for which we honor him today--Commander in Chief, Atlantic; Supreme Allied Commander, Atlantic, because in this capacity he has played a key role in building that great alliance of freedom-loving nations who have learned, I hope, the lessons of preparedness. Combining in himself the finest

qualities of the military man and the diplomat, Admiral Smith greatly strengthened the North Atlantic Treaty Organization and the bonds of friendship with our European allies."

Following his retirement, Admiral Smith was an active participant in fund raising activities to support local medical facilities, historical sites, and various charitable organizations. He married Helen Dee Rogers in Los Angeles on June 28, 1927. She was the last surviving allottee from the Osage enrollment of 1906.

Smith passed away while gardening at his home in Virginia Beach, Virginia on January 4, 1993 at the age of 88 and was buried at Woodlawn Memorial Gardens in Norfolk, Virginia.

U.S.S. MISSOURI

Captain William Brown

No one could have foreseen that when Captain William Brown took *Missouri* to sea for the first time following her refit at Norfolk that his first act as captain would be to run her aground in Chesapeake Bay resulting in a court-martial that would for all practical purposes end his career.

William Drane Brown was born in Punta Gorda, Florida on October 21, 1902 and attended Duval High School and the Marion Institute in Marion, Alabama before being appointed to the US Naval Academy from Florida on August 17, 1920 at the age of 17 years, 10 months.

While attending the academy, he spent 5 months at sea aboard the USS *Kansas* in 1921 and USS *Florida* in 1922. He played lacrosse and was on the varsity football team, playing in the 1923 Rose Bowl. He graduated 171 in a class of 545 on June 7, 1924 and was commissioned an ensign in the US Navy.

On June 24, 1924, he reported aboard the New Mexico-Class battleship USS *Mississippi* (BB-41) commissioned on December 18, 1917. Homeported in San Pedro, California, *Mississippi* left San Francisco on April 15, 1925 for war games held in the Territory of Hawaii, after which she went on a cruise to Australia, returning to California on September 26, to operate off the west coast.

U.S.S. MISSOURI

In 1926, Brown was under instruction at the submarine school at New London Connecticut and then was assigned duty aboard the submarine USS S-17 (SS-122). Operating out of at Mare Island in 1925 and 1926, she operated along the California coast in 1927, mainly at Mare Island, California, San Diego, California, and San Pedro, California.

In 1928, Brown returned to Annapolis to attend the Naval Postgraduate School, and upon graduating was assigned to the San Diego Naval Training Station training new sailors. In July 1933, Brown reported aboard the submarine USS S-28 (SS-133) as executive officer. The sub, formerly part of the Asiatic Fleet was transferred to Pearl Harbor in February 1931 where she'd remain for the next eight and a half years.

This duty was followed by an assignment teaching at the US Naval Academy from 1934-36, assigned to the Marine Engineering Department.

Brown returned to sea reporting aboard as executive officer of the newly-commissioned Porter-Class destroyer USS *Selfridge* (DD-357) on November 25, 1936, under the command of Commander, later Rear Admiral, Horace D. Clarke.

From January through February 1937, *Selfridge* conducted her shakedown cruise in the Mediterranean then returned to the east coast via the Caribbean in March. From April into August, she underwent her post-shakedown overhaul at Philadelphia, Pennsylvania after which she conducted training exercises in the area.

In September, she was assigned to Presidential escort duties at Poughkeepsie, New York; and, in October, she proceeded to Norfolk, Virginia, from where she got underway for the Panama Canal Zone and duty with the Battle Force in the Pacific. Diverted back to Norfolk for another Presidential escort mission in early November, she got underway again for the west coast on December 9, 1937.

Selfridge transited the Panama Canal and joined the Battle Force as flagship of Destroyer Squadron 4, (DESRON 4) on December 13, 1937 and reached San Diego, California on September 22. On October 1, 1938, Brown was promoted to lieutenant-commander.

Captain William Brown

Except for fleet problems and exercises, *Selfridge* remained in the southern California area for the next two years before being reassigned to Pearl Harbor in 1940. Brown left the ship in July 1940 to travel to Quincy Massachusetts to fit out and take command of the USS *Gregory* (APD-3). Originally commissioned as a Wickes-Class destroyer on June 1, 1918, with war in Europe threatening to involve the United States, *Gregory* and three other four-stackers were taken out of mothballs for conversion to high-speed fast transports.

The destroyers were stripped of virtually all their armament to make room for boats, while other important modifications were made for troops and cargo. *Gregory* was recommissioned on November 4, 1940 as APD-3 with Lt. Cmdr. Brown in command.

Gregory joined USS *Little* (DD-79 /APD-4), USS *Colhoun* (DD-85/APD-2), and USS *McKean* (DD-90/APD-5) to form Transport Division 12 (TRANSDIV 12). For the next year, *Gregory* and her sister APDs trained along the East Coast improving landing techniques with various Marine divisions. Subsequently, all but *McKean* would be lost during the Solomon Islands campaign.

On December 13, 1941, six days after the Japanese attack on Pearl Harbor, Brown left the *Gregory* to travel to Bath, Maine to fit out and take command of the Fletcher-Class destroyer USS *Nicolas* (DD-449) which was commissioned on June 4, 1942.

Nicholas was assigned to Destroyer Squadron 21 (DESRON 21), and departed New York City August 23, 1942, sailing with USS *Washington* (BB-56). They transited the Panama Canal, and continued on into the Central Pacific, arriving at Espiritu Santo on September 27. Three days later she began escorting Guadalcanal-bound troop and supply convoys.

Nicolas escorted the convoys assembled at Espiritu Santo and Nouméa to Guadalcanal and Tulagi, protected them as they off-loaded and then returned the vessels to their departure point. Periodically assigned to offensive duties she also conducted antisubmarine hunter-killer missions off Allied harbors, conducted sweeps of "the Slot" (New Georgia Sound) that runs down the center of the Solomon Islands, from Bougainville to Guadalcanal. She bombarded shore targets and performed gunfire missions in support of Marine and

Army units as they pushed toward the Tenamba River and total control of Guadalcanal.

In January 1943, *Nicholas* was part of Task Force 67 (TF-67) nicknamed the "Cactus Striking Force". The destroyers resisted the Japanese final counterattack for Guadalcanal by pounding the newly built enemy air facilities at Munda on January 4–5, then shelling their Kokumbona-Cape Esperance escape route on January 19. She bombarded the Japanese Munda resupply depot at Vila on Kolombangara on January 23–24. On January 26, 1943, Brown turned over command of the Nicolas to the executive officer, Lt. Comdr. Andrew J. Hill.

Later, the *Nicolas* would be awarded a Presidential Unit Citation for her actions at Kolombangora, Solomon Islands on the night of July 5, 1943, the citation stating:

"After waging a vigorous battle as part of the small Task Force which destroyed a superior Japanese surface force, the NICHOLAS remained behind with an accompanying destroyer to save the survivors of the torpedoed U.S.S. HELENA. Forced to clear the area on three occasions during rescue operations, she gallantly fought off continuing attacks by Japanese warships emerging from Kula Gulf and, with the other destroyer, sank or damaged an enemy light cruiser and two destroyers with deadly torpedo and gunfire, returning to the area after each onslaught to complete the heroic rescue of more than seven hundred survivors."

In February 1943, Brown reported as Chief of Staff to Rear Admiral A. S. Merrill, Commander Cruiser Division 12 (COMCRUDIV 12) and Task Group 36.9 (TG 36.9) as operations continued in the New Georgia area of the Solomon Islands. He was promoted to the temporary rank of captain on June 1, 1943.

From October 31 to November 3, 1943, Cruiser Division 12 operated as part of Task Force 68 and later Task Force 39, and Brown would be awarded two Legion of Merit Medals for his work as chief of staff, the first for *"his clear logical thinking while under fire"* at Kolombangara in March 1943, and the second award for his work as operations officer for TF-39, the citation stating that TF-39, and Brown:

"Decisively defeated in night action, a heavier gunned enemy surface force composed of at least four cruisers, of which two were 8-inch cruisers, and eight

destroyers of which at least one cruiser and four destroyers were sunk and the remainder put to ignominious flight towards their bases with two cruisers and two destroyers heavily damaged and under hot pursuit by our forces.

This defeat prevented the Japanese Task Force from bombarding our beachhead at Empress Augusta Bay, and destroying our transport and minelaying groups and thereby materially contributed to the successful establishment of our land and air forces on Bougainville Island. -Successfully fought off a heavy air attack by at least 67 Japanese dive and medium bombers with the destruction of at least 17 Japanese planes by the ships' anti-aircraft gunfire."

In January 1944, Brown was back in Washington DC, assigned to the staff of Admiral Ernest King, the Commander in Chief United States Fleet and also Chief of Naval Operations, and exercised operational command over the Atlantic, Pacific, and Asiatic Fleets, as well as all naval coastal forces.

A year later, in January 1945, Brown was Commander Destroyer Squadron 62 (COMDESRON 62) then served as Chief of Staff to Commander Destroyer Pacific Fleet. This was followed by a tour as Commanding Officer of the Naval Mine Countermeasures Station at Panama City Florida.

When Captain Brown relieved Captain Harold P. Smith on December 10, 1949, the *Missouri* was still being overhauled at the Norfolk Naval Shipyard. It was Brown's first time at sea since the end of the war, and the largest ship he'd ever commanded.

On December 23, following her refit, Brown took the Missouri out for a brief trip around the Virginia capes and she returned to Norfolk on Christmas Eve. Her next scheduled departure was for January 17, at which time *Missouri* was to sail to Guantanamo Bay for maneuvers.

On January 13, Brown was requested by the Naval Ordnance Laboratory for the *Missouri* to proceed through a channel in which the Navy had strewn acoustic cables as part of an ongoing project that aimed to identify ships by their propeller signatures. The request was entirely optional, but as the captain was preoccupied with the details of the upcoming journey to Cuba, he gave the letter little attention and instead referred the matter to his operations officer, Commander John

R. Millett, who in turn referred the letter to the ship's navigator, Lieutenant Commander Frank G. Morris.

This run was a last-minute addition to the plan, and the range itself, while deep enough to take the battleship, was dangerously close to shallow water. Worse, three of the five buoys which had previously marked the range had recently been removed, and the charts onboard had yet to be updated to reflect this. Some members of the crew knew this, but there was a communication breakdown, and Brown was not made aware of this.

When the *Missouri* sailed on January 17th, she was fully loaded with ammunition, fuel, and supplies. As the ship headed for the acoustic range, the situation aboard was confused. Several key officers had only learned of the run through the range after the ship had sailed, and Brown moved between the bridge and the chart room, interrupting the routine in both spaces.

As *Missouri* began to leave Hampton Roads, it was only near Fort Wool that Brown told his officers about the acoustic test. The officers appeared confused at this news. The ocean current was strong that morning, so the ship's speed was increased to 15 knots.

When the buoy marking the left edge of the range was spotted, Brown assumed it was the marker for the right edge of the range, and steered to the left of it, mistaking the buoys for a fishing channel for the missing markers. This took *Missouri* into shoal water, which didn't go unnoticed. Brown ignored the navigator's warnings, at one point accusing him of not knowing where they were.

Too late, Brown realized the mistake and ordered a course change, but it was too late, and *Missouri* hit Thimble Shoal at 8:17 am, the momentum driving her 2,500 feet onto the sandbar and lifting her several feet out of the water. Brown ordered the engines reversed in an attempt to pull her off, but she was firmly wedged, and the engines had to be shut down as sand clogged the condensers. This same problem affected the generators, so power was quickly lost throughout the ship.

More embarrassing, the sandbar was within plain sight of "Admirals Row", the homes along Dillingham Boulevard at Naval Station Norfolk occupied by 18 flag officers of the Navy stationed at

Hampton Roads, and the homes of a similar number of high-ranking officers of the United States Army stationed at Fort Monroe.

It took two weeks and 23 vessels, but on February 1, Missouri was finally freed and as the ship's band played the Missouri Waltz, Anchors Aweigh, and Nobody Knows the Trouble I've Seen, the *Missouri*'s crew ran up their largest battle flags, and signal halyards spelling out "Reporting For Duty as she was towed back to the naval yard to undergo repairs, which included replacement of some of her double-bottom plating that had buckled and ruptured three fuel tanks. Two days later, on February 3, Brown was relieved of command by Commander George E. Peckham.

Three and a half months after running the *Missouri* aground, Brown and three other officers were brought before a court-martial. Brown initially tried to blame his subordinates, but when this proved unpopular with the court, he accepted blame and plead guilty to neglect of duty and negligence. He was reduced 250 places on the Navy's list of captains, effectively ending his career.

Two of the other officers, Lt. Cmdr. Morris, the navigator and Cmdr. Millet, the operations officer, were also reduced on the promotion list, while the CIC officer, Lieutenant John Carr, received a letter of reprimand.

Brown served briefly on the staff of Commander Submarine Group 5 (COMSUBGRU 5) and with the Florida Group Atlantic Reserve Fleet, before retiring from active duty on June 30, 1955, with a promotion to rear admiral on the retired list.

Brown retired to Gainesville, Florida, where he passed away at the Gainesville Medical Center Hospital on January 11, 1991. He was interred with full military honors at Arlington National Cemetery on January 28, 1991.

Captain George E. Peckham

Commander George E. Peckham's period of time in command of the *Missouri* consisted of seventy-six hours, from the time Captain Brown left on February 3, 1950 until February 7, when Captain Smith returned to again take command of the revered battleship. But it would be his command of destroyers that he would be recognized and remembered for.

George Edward Peckham was born November 27, 1908 in Cresco, a small rural town in northeast Iowa that despite a population of only 4,000 in 2010 boasts a number of notable residents including Nobel Laureate Norman Borlaug, Medal of Honor recipient Edouard Izac, five WW II admirals, and Ellen Church, the world's first flight attendant.

Raised by his grandparents, he was appointed to the US Naval Academy from the state of Iowa on June 17, 1927. "Peck" as he was known to other midshipmen, was a Cadet 1st Class Petty Officer and he graduated 147 in a class of 443 on June 4, 1931 and was commissioned an ensign in the US Navy.

Peckham's first assignment was aboard the Omaha-class light cruiser USS *Cincinnati* (CL-6), originally referred to as a scout cruiser. Assigned to the Scouting Fleet, she operated exclusively in the Atlantic and Caribbean.

In 1934, with a promotion to Lieutenant junior-grade, Peckham served aboard the USS *Boggs* (DD-136) a Wickes-Class destroyer commissioned on September 23, 1918 at the Mare Island Navy Yard with Commander H. V. McKittrick in command.

Boggs served with the Pacific Fleet until being placed out of commission on June 29, 1922. She was re-commissioned on September 5, 1931 and re-designated a miscellaneous auxiliary (AG-19). On December 19, 1931 she was assigned to Mobile Target Division 1, Battle Force, for high-speed radio control tests, target towing, and minesweeping duties. Peckham served as engineering officer until transferring to the USS *Overton* (DD-239) in 1935.

The *Overton* was a Clemson-class destroyer and high-speed transport that was commissioned on June 30, 1920. In 1932, because of budgetary restrictions caused by the Great Depression, she was placed in rotating reserve commission, where vessels were inactive for six months, then active for twelve months, and she served in that capacity until again decommissioned, in reserve, on November 20, 1937.

In 1938, Peckham was assigned to the Philadelphia Navy Yard where he was assigned to the Industrial Department and he later reported aboard the newly commissioned USS *Buck* (DD-420), a Wickes-Class destroyer. Peckham reported as gunnery officer and was promoted to lieutenant on May 1, 1939. That same year, records show he attended Stanford University, earning a Masters' Degree in Education in 1941, followed by attendance at the Army War College at Carlisle Barracks, Pennsylvania from 1941-42.

In the early part of 1943, Peckham, promoted to the temporary rank of commander, was awarded the Silver Star Medal:

"for conspicuous gallantry and intrepidity as Operations Officer on the Staff of the Commander of a Destroyer Squadron in action against enemy Japanese forces during World War II. During a fierce, prolonged engagement with numerically superior hostile surface units, Commander Peckham rendered invaluable services by skillfully evaluating the tactical situation and accurately transmitting the orders of his Squadron Commander, despite persistent and determined heavy enemy gunfire. His expert professional ability and sound judgment contributed materially to the success of our forces."

CAPTAIN GEORGE E. PECKHAM

On October 3, 1943, Peckham took command of the USS *Selfridge* (DD-357), a Porter-Class destroyer commissioned on November 25, 1936. In May 1943, *Selfridge* was assigned to the 3rd Fleet, arriving at Nouméa, New Caledonia on May 12. Through the summer, she operated with cruisers of TF-36, later TF-37, and in late September, as a unit of the 3rd Fleet's amphibious force, she escorted an LST convoy to Vella Lavella, in the Solomon Islands then commenced nighttime patrols through "the Slot" to intercept Japanese shipping.

On the night of October 6, 1943, three days after relieving Lt. Commander Carroll D. Reynolds, *Selfridge,* and two other destroyers, USS *O'Bannon* (DD-450), and USS *Chevalier* (DD-451) intercepted a Japanese force of six destroyers, three destroyer transports, and smaller armed craft some 12 miles off Marquana Bay as they attempted to evacuate land forces from Vella Lavella.

In the ensuing Battle of Vella Lavella, *Chevalier* was torpedoed and damaged beyond repair. *Selfridge* and *O'Bannon* were both heavily damaged in action, *Selfridge* by an enemy torpedo, *O'Bannon* by enemy fire compounded by collision with *Chevalier* just after the latter had gone dead in the water. The enemy retired with three newly arrived American destroyers in pursuit, while *O'Bannon* guarded her stricken sisters, rescuing the survivors of *Chevalier.* For his actions, Peckham was awarded a second Silver Star Medal, the citation reading:

"Assigned the hazardous task of intercepting and preventing an attempt by hostile forces to evacuate beleaguered Japanese troops from the area, Commander Peckham fearlessly sought out and engaged nine enemy ships, closing immediately to 7,000 yards, and delivering a devastating torpedo attack followed by accurate and

effective gunfire. When the other two vessels of his small squadron were severely damaged in the furious battle and compelled to withdraw, he courageously continued directing the gallant efforts of his ship until the enemy was repulsed and, although the heavily damaged SELFRIDGE was in danger of capsizing and sinking, he and his heroic crew worked tirelessly in the efficient execution of damage control measures and brought the ship safely to port. By his expert tactical knowledge and inspiring leadership in the face of overwhelming odds, Commander Peckham greatly contributed to the sinking of one or more hostile vessels and the damaging of three others."

Chevalier was sunk the following day by a torpedo from USS *La Vallette* (DD- 448). *Chevalier* lost 54 killed. Casualties on board *Selfridge* amounted to 13 killed, 11 wounded, and 36 missing. The *O' Bannon* would go on to become the Navy's most decorated destroyer during World War II, earning 17 battle stars and a Presidential Unit Citation.

After temporary repairs were made at Purvis Bay and at Nouméa, *Selfridge* sailed to Mare Island Naval Shipyard for permanent repairs, including the installation of a new bow and a completely new gun armament, but when, after refresher training out of San Diego, she returned to Pearl Harbor on May 10, 1944, she would be under the command of Lt. Cmdr. Lewis Levi Snider, who relieved Peckham on February 9.

On June 7, 1944, the USS *Waldron* (DD-699) was commissioned at the New York Navy Yard with Commander Peckham in command. Following her shakedown cruise in the vicinity of Bermuda during the early summer of 1944, she returned to New York from July 22 until August 6 and then headed back to the Bermuda area for further training.

Waldron returned to New York in mid-September but got underway again on September 26 and transited the Panama Canal on October 1 to report for duty with the Pacific Fleet. She departed Balboa on October 4 and after a brief stop at San Pedro, California from October 12 to 14, she arrived at Pearl Harbor on October 20. She remained in the Hawaiian Islands until December 17, then departed for the western Pacific.

She arrived at Ulithi lagoon in the Caroline Islands on December 28, 1944 and was assigned duty in the screen of the Fast Carrier Task Force (TF-38 when assigned to the Third Fleet and TF-58 when serving with the Fifth Fleet). *Waldron* departed Ulithi with TF 38 on December 30, assigned to Destroyer Squadron 62 (DESRON 62) comprised of nine destroyers in two divisions.

Destroyer Division 123 (DESRON 123), under the command of Captain J. M. Higgins, included the USS *English* (DD 696), flaghip, USS *Charles S. Sperry* (DD 697), USS *Ault* (DD 698), USS *Waldron* (DD 699) and USS *Haynsworth* (DD 700).

Destroyer Division 124 (DESRON 124) included USS *John W. Weeks* (DD 701), USS *Hank* (DD 702), USS *Wallace L. Lind* (DD 703) and USS *Borie* (DD 704).

The destroyers protected the carriers while they launched their planes against enemy installations on January 3 and 4, 1945 and again on January 6 and 7, her carriers aircraft pounded targets on the island of Luzon. Both raids were part of the preparations for the amphibious assault on Luzon carried out at Lingayen Gulf on January 9.

As the troops stormed ashore there, however, *Waldron* and the carriers returned north to suppress enemy air power on Formosa during the actual assault. That same day, she steamed through Bashi Channel into the South China Sea with TF 38 to begin a series of raids on Japan's inner defenses.

Their first assault was at Cam Ranh Bay in Indochina, where Admiral Halsey hoped to find Japanese battleships *Ise* and *Hyūga*, however the two Japanese warships had moved south to safer waters at Singapore. The raids commenced forward on January 12, with naval aviators sinking 44 ships, 15 of which were Japanese warships and the remainder being merchant ships.

U.S.S. MISSOURI

After fueling on January 13, TF 38, with *Waldron* still screening the force, carried out air attacks on Hainan Island and on Hong Kong. The following day, the planes of TF-38 returned to Formosa for antishipping sweeps and attacks on the Formosa airfields.

On January 16, the carriers again launched their planes against Hainan and Hong Kong. Late on the night of January 20, *Waldron*, the antimine and antisubmarine patrol, led TF-38 out of the South China Sea through Balintang Channel and into the Philippine Sea. The destroyer and her carriers returned to their base at Ulithi on the 26th after conducting strikes on Formosa and on Okinawa.

Waldron departed Ulithi on February 10 accompanying TF-58, this time to support the assault on Iwo Jima scheduled for February 19. In support, the carriers planned to carry out the first carrier-based air strikes on Japan since the Doolittle Raid of 1942. On February 16 and 17, the carriers of TF-58 sent their aircraft aloft for raids on the Tokyo area of Honshū. The task force then sailed to Iwo Jima to provide air support for the following day's invasion.

On the night of 17/18 February, *Waldron*'s task group encountered several small Japanese patrol craft. One of the crafts attacked the USS *Dortch* (DD-670) with her 3-inch guns, killing three of the destroyer's crewmen. Due to darkness and the proximity of *Dortch* and the *Charles S. Sperry*, *Waldron* could not bring her battery to bear. Instead, she laid on a course for the enemy craft and charged her at 21 knots. At about 5 am on February 18, *Waldron* rammed the Japanese picket boat amidships and cut her neatly in two. About four hours later, the destroyer received orders detaching her from TF-58 to head for Saipan and repairs to her bow.

Peckham was awarded a third Silver Star for the action, the citation stating:

"for conspicuous gallantry and intrepidity as Commanding Officer of the Destroyer U.S.S. WALDRON (DD-699), in action against enemy forces in Japanese home waters, from 10 February to 4 March 1945. Skillfully maneuvering his ship in the darkness on 18 February, Commander Peckham rammed and destroyed an enemy picket boat attempting to penetrate the destroyer screen, thereby contributing materially to the protection of the Task Group and the resultant success of the operation."

Arriving at Saipan on February 20, *Waldron* underwent repairs and departed Saipan in the afternoon of February 23. Upon arrival off Iwo Jima on February 25, *Waldron* reported to TF-51 for temporary duty with the transport screen. During that assignment, she also provided naval gunfire support for the troops operating ashore on February 26 and 27. On the 27th, *Waldron* rejoined the screen of TG-58.3. After an air strike on Okinawa on March 1, she returned to Ulithi with the carriers, arriving there on March 4.

On March 14, *Waldron* again departed for the Japanese home islands with the fast carriers, arriving in Japanese home waters on March 18 to begin launching strikes on Kyushu airfields the same day. Later that day, the enemy counterattacked with kamikazes and succeeded in hitting the aircraft carrier USS *Franklin* (CV-13). Waldron was one of the ships assigned to cover the severely damaged carrier during the initial stage of her withdrawal from action.

Antiaircraft action continued throughout the three days *Waldron* provided escort for *Franklin*; and, on the night of March 20 /21, the *Waldron* scored a kill of her own when her radar-directed main battery brought down a Japanese Yokosuka D4Y "*Judy.*" She took another intruder under fire briefly that night, but technical problems prevented a second kill. On March 22, she rejoined the main carrier force and resumed her screening duties while the planes struck at Okinawa and Kyushu in preparation for the invasion of Okinawa.

For the next three months, *Waldron* continued to screen the carriers during their support missions for the Okinawa campaign. During that time, she was engaged in a number of antiaircraft actions and participated in two shore bombardments of air installations on Minami Daito Shima. The one antiaircraft action which resulted in a definite kill for the destroyer occurred on May 14, although she claimed four sure assists in addition during that period.

On May 26, she departed the Ryukyu Islands with her task group and, on June 1, arrived at San Pedro Bay, Leyte and remained there until July 1 at which time she returned to sea with TF 38. For the remainder of the war, she remained with the fast carriers during the final strikes on the Japanese home islands.

The end of hostilities on August 15 found *Waldron* off the Japanese coast with TF 38. She screened the carriers while their aircraft covered the initial occupation of Japan. That duty lasted until September 10, after which she finally entered Tokyo Bay.

Waldron remained supporting the American occupation forces until November 4, when she departed Okinawa, bound for home, after stops at Eniwetok and Pearl Harbor. On November 11, Peckham turned command of *Waldron* over to Commander Theodore A. Torgerson.

In 1949, he reported aboard the *Missouri*, and briefly commanded her before returning command to Capt. Harold Smith on February 7, 1950. In 1952, he was head of the Mobilization Plans and Policy Branch in the Office of the Chief of Naval Operations in Washington DC.

Peckham took command of USS *Menifee* (APA-202), a Haskell-class attack transport, on September 23, 1953 relieving Captain James T. Smith. During her deployment to the Western Pacific from August 1953 to April 1954, Peckham, now a captain, took part in extensive amphibious training exercises with American and Korean Marines and *Menifee* served as the flagship for Operation *"Big Lift"*, the transfer of neutral Indian troops to the peace conference in Panmunjom.

USS FREMONT (APA-44)

On August 29, 1957, Peckham took command of Amphibious Squadron 8 (TRANSPHIBRON 8) later (PHIBRON 8) aboard his flagship USS *Fremont* (APA-44) a WW II era Bayfield-class attack transport. She operated primarily in the Mediterranean, and in September 1958, transported the 6th Marines to Beirut, Lebanon. Late in 1958, Peckham took command of Amphibious Training Atlantic (COMPHIBTRALANT) until his retirement in October 1959. He was promoted to rear admiral during the ceremony held at the amphibious naval base at Little Creek, Norfolk, Virginia.

He and his wife Marie Agnes retired to Falls Church, Virginia and he passed away on September 14, 1998. He was laid to rest with full military honors at Barrancas National Cemetery, Pensacola, Florida.

U.S.S. MISSOURI

Captain Irving T. Duke

Captain Irving Duke was already a combat veteran when he took command of the *Missouri* in 1950. Under his command, Duke would take her to her second war during the conflict in Korea.

Irving Terrill Duke was born in Richmond City, Virginia on January 9, 1901 to Walter Garland Duke, a prominent attorney and his wife Jane Henderson Duke, whose family roots date back to colonial Virginia.

Duke, an excellent student, graduated Richmond High School with a scholarship to the University of Richmond, but instead was appointed to the US Naval Academy by Virginia Senator Claude A. Swanson, and he entered the academy on June 16, 1920. "Irv", as he was known, graduated 4th in a class of 525 in June 1924 and was commissioned an ensign.

On July 7, 1924, Duke reported aboard the battleship USS *Tennessee* (BB-43) the lead ship of the Tennessee-Class of dreadnought battleships, commissioned in June 1920. Under the command of Captain Luke McNamee, the *Tennessee* operated as part of the Battle Fleet, operating in the Pacific. Besides the routine fleet training exercises and annual Fleet Problems, Duke was aboard for the goodwill cruises to Australia and New Zealand in 1925.

The fleet returned to San Pedro in September 1925, followed by a three-month visit to Hawaii in April 1927. In 1928, she had a crane and an aircraft catapult on her fantail to accommodate reconnaissance floatplanes. Promoted to lieutenant (jg) while aboard, Duke left the ship in 1928.

Duke attended Submarine School at New London, Connecticut in 1928, and after graduation, he spent three years serving aboard the submarine USS -48 (SS-159). On June 1, 1929, S-48 was assigned to Submarine Division 4 (SUBDIV 4), with which she operated through the end of 1929. Then assigned to SUBDIV 3, later SUBDIV 5, and then Squadron 3, she continued her operations off the New England coast, with an interruption for winter maneuvers to the south. During this time, Lieutenant Hyman G. Rickover, "Father of the Nuclear Navy" was also assigned aboard.

In 1931, Duke reported for instruction at the Naval Postgraduate School at Annapolis, Maryland. He was promoted to lieutenant on June 30, 1932 and he graduated with an advanced degree in General Ordnance in 1934.

From 1934-1937, Duke served aboard the newly commissioned USS *Tuscaloosa* (CA-37) a New Orleans-class cruiser commissioned in 1934. Duke was assigned as the assistant gunnery officer and the ship, based at San Pedro, California operated primarily in the Atlantic and Caribbean. As part of Cruiser Division 6 (CRUDIV 6) she participated in Fleet Problem XVII in Panama (1936) and Fleet Problem XVIII in Alaska (1937).

In 1937, Duke had shore duty assigned to the Naval Proving Ground at Dahlgren, Virginia, assigned as a Battery Officer, where he was promoted to lieutenant commander on July 1, 1938. On June 16, 1939, Duke returned to the sea, assigned to fit out the USS *Helena* (CL-50) a Brooklyn-class light cruiser under construction in Brooklyn and reported aboard after she was commissioned on September 18, 1939.

World War II had broken out in Europe in September of that year, but the United States remained neutral and the ship was occupied with sea trials and initial training, and she embarked on a major shakedown cruise abroad on December 27, bound for South American waters.

After stopping at Guantanamo Bay Naval Base in Cuba, she proceeded to Buenos Aires, Argentina, arriving on January 22, 1940, then continued on to Montevideo, Uruguay on January 29. While in the latter port, the crew inspected the wreck of the German heavy cruiser Admiral *Graf Spee* that had recently been scuttled after the Battle of the River Plate the previous month. Helena got underway again in mid-February to return to the United States, again passing through Guantanamo Bay on the way.

After returning, she was dry-docked for repairs from March 2 through July 20. She took part in training exercises and sea trials over the next several months until September, when she was transferred to the Pacific Fleet. Duke left the ship in September 1940, eventually taking command of the newly commissioned USS *Mayo* (DD-442) a Benson-class destroyer commissioned on September 18, 1940.

Following her shakedown cruise, *Mayo* joined the expanding Neutrality Patrol after shakedown and escorted the first Marines to Iceland on July 7, 1941 as they took protective custody of that key island. As President Franklin D. Roosevelt and British Prime Minister Winston Churchill agreed to the Atlantic Charter during the second week in August, *Mayo* guarded their meeting by patrolling off NS Argentia, Newfoundland.

The entry of the United States into World War II lengthened her convoy assignment beyond the western Atlantic Ocean. Escort of slow merchant convoys out of Boston gave way in summer 1942 to duty with fast troop transports out of New York City, but U-boats and bad weather were not the only dangers.

On August 27, 1942, *Mayo* departed the Clyde estuary in Scotland as part of Convoy TA-18, escorting vessels bound for New York. On the evening of September 3, a fire broke out deep within the bowels of the troop transport USS *Wakefield* (AP-21) and spread rapidly. *Wakefield* swung to port to run before the wind while fire-fighting began immediately.

Ammunition was thrown overboard to prevent its detonation, code room publications were secured, and sick bay and brig inmates were released. *Mayo* and the cruiser *Brooklyn* (CL-40) closed to windward to take off passengers, a badly-burned officer, and members of the crew not needed to man pumps and hoses. Other survivors were disembarked by boat and raft, to be picked up by the other screening ships. Filipino Ship's Steward 1st Class Francisco Siladio was the only Coast Guardsman killed in the fire.

U.S.S. MISSOURI

Mayo removed 247 survivors and for his efforts in coordinating rescue operations, Duke was awarded the Navy and Marine Corps Medal for the rescue and cited for *"heroism and outstanding performance of duty."*

During May through August of 1943, Duke served on the staff of Rear Admiral Francis W. Rockwell, Commander 9th Amphibious Force as operations officer of the joint Army-Navy staff during the planning for the invasion of Attu and Kiska in the Aleutian Islands, and then as operations officer on the staff of the assault force. Future Missouri captain, Robert Dennison served as Rockwell's chief of staff. Duke was awarded the Legion of Merit, the citation stating he *"coordinated the movements of various elements of the assault force"* substantially contributing to the success of the operation. On June 1, 1943, Duke was advanced to the rank of temporary captain.

In January 1944, Duke was ordered to Washington DC to supervise the Design and Drafting Section of the Naval Gun Factory where he finished the war. In January 1946, he was on the staff of Vice Admiral Frederick C. Sherman, Commander 5th Fleet aboard the flagship USS *Iowa* (BB-61) at Yokosuka, Japan. Upon his return to San Diego, he served on the staff of Vice Admiral Alfred E. Montgomery.

Photo # 80-G-414591 USS Missouri change of command. April 1950

On December 21, 1949, Duke relieved Captain Joseph M. Worthington to take command of the Oregon-Class heavy cruiser USS *Rochester* (CA-124) which he briefly commanded until March 29, 1950 when he was relieved by Captain Edward L. Lender. During that time, he sailed her from her overhaul at the South Boston Naval Yard to her new homeport in Long Beach, California. On April 19, 1950, following the outbreak of war in Korea, Duke relieved Capt. Smith to take command of the *Missouri*. As part of the naval mobilization *Missouri* was called up

108

from the Atlantic Fleet where she was training midshipmen and departed Norfolk on August 19 to support UN forces in Korea.

Missouri arrived west of Kyūshū on September 14 and was assigned as the flagship of Rear Admiral Allan Edward Smith. The first American battleship to reach Korean waters, she bombarded Samchok on September 15, 1950 in an attempt to divert troops and attention away from the Incheon landings, firing fifty-two 16" projectiles, damaging two railroad bridges. In the following days, Missouri would conduct shore bombardments along the coast, this time at Pohang, before returning to Japan for supplies.

She returned to Korea off Inchon on September 19, but hurricanes and poor weather resulted in Missouri arriving too late to support the Inchon landings that led to the recapture of Seoul, but she was able to fire shore bombardments that targeted enemy combatants on the road from Suwon to Seoul.

**Marilyn Maxwell, Bob Hope and Adm. Struble
aboard the Missouri**

In October, USS Missouri became the flagship of Vice Admiral Arthur D. Struble, Commander Seventh Fleet. On October 12, she bombed the Mitsubishi Iron Works, reportedly firing 96 rounds from her main battery in under an hour. On October 13, she bombarded

Tanchon. On October 26, she supported the amphibious landing of Wonsan. The next day on October 27, Bob Hope and Marilyn Maxwell celebrated Navy Day on board, performing three shows that day: one for the enlisted, one for the officers, and again for those who had missed the original performances.

By late October, UN forces had pushed North Korean forces back into North Korea beyond the 38th parallel, prompting intervention from Communist China and the Soviet Union, which in turn drove UN forces south again. Battleship *Missouri* was at Hungnam where Marines were retreating from Chosin Reservoir in December, providing a curtain of fire for the evacuating Marines, sailing with Task Group 90.8 under the leadership of Rear Admiral Roscoe Hillenkoetter, one of *Missouri's* former commanding officers.

Missouri conducted additional operations with carriers and shore bombardments off the east coast of Korea until March 19, 1951, after which she arrived at Yokosuka, on March 24, where Duke was relieved by Captain George T. Wright.

She departed Yokosuka on March 28, and, via Hawaii and the Panama Canal, arrival at Norfolk on April 27 became the flagship of Rear Admiral James Holloway, the commander of Cruiser Force, Atlantic Fleet.

From June 1951 through July 1952 Duke was commanding officer of the Naval Proving Ground at Dahlgren, Virginia, then in July 1952, he took command the Key West Naval Base in Florida with a promotion to rear admiral on May 7, 1953.

In July 1953, he was assigned to the Office of the Chief of Naval Operations as Director of Fleet Development and Maintenance, then as the Director of Undersea Warfare from 1954-55. On May 26,

1955, he relieved Captain Walter Winn, acting as the temporary Commander Amphibious Group 1 (COMPHIBGRU 1), who then served as Duke's Chief of Staff.

Duke finished his career as Assistant Chief of Naval Operations before retiring from active duty in 1961, with a promotion to vice-admiral. After retiring from the navy, Duke spent 13 years as resident superintendent of the Robert E. Lee Foundation at Stratford Hall in Westmoreland County, Va.

Duke married Helen Shannon in Los Angeles on September 16, 1927 with whom he had a daughter, Terrill in 1931. Duke died in a Frederick Hospital of cardiac arrest on November 30, 1979 and was buried in Arlington National Cemetery with full military honors on December 4, 1979.

U.S.S. MISSOURI

Captain George C. Wright

Captain George C. Wright took command of the *Missouri* at Yokosuka, Japan, on March 2, 1951 and by the end of the month he would sail her away from her first Korean deployment to return to the United States, via Hawaii. But not before commanding her in combat.

Missouri continued to conduct shore bombardments of Korea's eastern coast and provided cover for aircraft carriers in Task Force 77 until March 19 and she returned to Yokosuka on March 24, departing four days later. For his actions, Wright would be awarded a second Bronze Star Medal.

George Charles Wright was born in New Hampton, Iowa, on August 3, 1902, the second son of George Cyrus and Mary Jane (Hamilton) Wright. He and his older brother Carleton Herbert, ten years his senior, were orphaned by their parent's early death, and their Uncle, James Lloyd Wright, a Washington DC newspaper correspondent was named as guardian.

Wright was raised in Denver, Colorado and Buffalo, New York and Washington, D. C. where he attended public schools. Wright was appointed to the U. S. Naval Academy from the Twentieth District of Ohio by Rep. Chas A. Mooney on June 24, 1921.

The Naval Academy's Lucky Bag magazine described Wright, nicknamed "Commander" as having a "strong back and weak mind" no doubt referring to his prowess at football but less than stellar academic achievement, except for demonstrating an aptitude for Naval Engineering. He sailed aboard the USS *Wyoming* for his summer cruise and graduated 115 out of a class of 457 on June 4, 1925, with a commission as an ensign in the US Navy, and a BS in science granted retroactively in 1938, due to a law passed in 1937.

After a brief tour of duty with the Division of Fleet Training at the Navy Department in Washington DC, Wright reported aboard the battleship USS *New York* (BB-34), the flagship of Battleship Division 2, Scouting Fleet. Wright received a letter of commendation when the *New York* finished first place in the 1925 fleet gunnery competition.

In September 1926, aboard the USS *Lamson* (DD-328) a Clemson-Class destroyer commission on April 19, 1921. The *Lamson* was flagship for Destroyer Division 27 (DESDIV 7) as part of Destroyer Squadron 9 (DESRON 9). Assigned to the U.S. Naval Forces in Europe, *Lamson* departed Boston, Massachusetts on June 18, 1925 for operations in European and Mediterranean waters. Returning to the United States a year later.

From January 3 through June 16, 1927, Wright was detached from the *Lamson* to attend the Navy Torpedo School at Newport, Rhode Island. *Lamson,* part of the Scouting Fleet, participated in exercises and maneuvers along the Atlantic coast and in the Caribbean and Wright remained aboard until she was decommissioned at Philadelphia on May 1, 1930.

That May, Wright reported for instruction at the Naval Postgraduate School at Newport, R.I. and graduated in June 1932 with a Masters' Degree in Mechanical Engineering from Columbia University in New York. Upon graduation, Wright reported aboard the battleship USS *Pennsylvania* (BB-38) later that June.

Pennsylvania served as the flagship of Admiral Frank H. Schofield, Commander in Chief US Fleet (CINCUS) ironically produced "sink us". Originally homeported at San Pedro, California she cruised the California coat until November when she returned to San Pedro going inactive until early March 1934.

After a short visit to Hunters Point Naval Shipyard in San Francisco, and then she went to join the fleet for Fleet Problem XV, which was held in the Caribbean. She passed through the canal on April 24, the maneuvers having already started on the 19th. They lasted until 12 May, at which point Pennsylvania returned to New York.

In New York, *Pennsylvania* led the fleet in a naval review for President Franklin D. Roosevelt. On June 15, 1934, Admiral Joseph M. Reeves took command of the fleet aboard *Pennsylvania*, which was once again the fleet flagship. Returning to San Pedro on July 7, she sailed up the coast to Puget Sound, Washington for a refit that lasted from July 14 until October 2. The ship left the shipyard on October 16 and returned to San Francisco two days later, beginning a period of cruises off the coast of California.

Pennsylvania ended the year in San Pedro, remaining there until April 29, 1935, when she took part in Fleet Problem XVI in the Hawaiian Islands. During his time aboard, Wright received 2 letters of commendation for *Pennsylvania* coming in second place in both the 1934 and 1935 Fleet Engineering competition.

On June 28, 1935, Wright was appointed Shop Manager at the Naval Research Laboratory, Bellevue, Washington DC. Where he remained until December1, 1936, followed by an assignment as an aide and flag secretary to Commander Cruiser Division 6 (COMCRUDIV 6).

In June 1938, Wright reported aboard the Mahan-Class destroyer USS *Cummings* (DD-365) as executive officer. The Cummings was commissioned on November 25, 1936, with Commander C. P. Cecil in command, and departed New York on September 29, 1937 to join the Battle Fleet. She arrived at San Diego on October 28, 1937. Wright joined the ship shortly after its return from Hawaii and was aboard for the Presidential Fleet Review at San Francisco in July.

In 1939, fleet exercises were held in the Panama Canal Zone and the Caribbean from January to April and returning to San Diego on May 12, 1939. Wright was promoted to Lt. Commander on August 1, 1939, just prior to his leaving the *Cummings* and reporting to the Naval Academy on August 18, 1939 as an instructor in Marine Engineering. He finished the term on July 15, 1940 and he took command of the Wickes-Class destroyer USS *Bernadou* (DD-153) three days later on July 18, 1940.

U.S.S. MISSOURI

With war in Europe since September 1939, *Bernadou* which had been out of service from September 1936 through October 1939. She rejoined the fleet for service with Destroyer Division 6, (DESDIV 6) Atlantic Squadron, on Neutrality Patrol.

Following the French and English declaration of war on the Axis powers, the Chief of Naval Operations (CNO) established a combined air and ship patrol of the United States Atlantic coast, including the Caribbean, on September 4. President Roosevelt declared the United States neutral on September 5 and instituted the naval patrol, a Neutrality Patrol.

Roosevelt's initiation of the Neutrality Patrol, which in fact also escorted British ships, as well as orders to U.S. Navy destroyers first to actively report U-boats, then "shoot on sight", meant American neutrality was honored more in theory than in practice. Additionally, there was the ever-present risk of contact with potential belligerent vessels. Wright was relieved by Lt. Commander Robert E. Braddy Jr. on October 21, 1941.

On January 13, 1942, with the United States at war since December 7, Wright took command of the Porter-Class destroyer USS *McDougal* (DD-358) commissioned December 23, 1936. She was working convoy escort duty in the South Atlantic when she learned of the Japanese attack on Pearl Harbor.

After relieving Commander Dashiell Livingston Madeira at Trinidad on January 13, 1942, Wright and *McDougal* departed for patrol duty on January 18, 1942 off the South American coast. During the next several months she carried out patrol and escort duty between

Brazilian and Caribbean ports and following an overhaul at Charleston, South Carolina during July and August, she cruised via Caribbean ports to the Panama Canal where she arrived August 31.

Assigned to the Southeast Pacific Force, *McDougal* patrolled along the Pacific coast of Latin America beginning September 7, cruising out of Balboa, Panama Canal Zone, north to Nicaragua and south to the Straits of Magellan. She patrolled the southeast Pacific westward to the Galápagos and Juan Fernández Islands and touched coastal ports in Ecuador, Peru, and Chile. While aboard the *McDougal,* Wright was promoted to Temporary Commander on August 1, 1942 and Temporary Captain on July 20, 1943.

On August 12, 1943, Captain Wright was detached from *McDougal* to take command of Destroyer Division 21 (DESDIV 21) and he was awarded a Bronze Star Medal with Combat V for his actions in command during anti-submarine operations off Santa Pola, Spain, on May 17, 1944, the citation stating:

"Temporarily embarked in the USS GLEAVES, {he) skillfully operated his section, hunting out and destroying an enemy submarine which had attacked an Allied convoy. During a three-day search for the enemy, he effectively coordinated the movements of his ship, finally attacking and destroying the undersea craft. His initiative, able leadership, and outstanding devotion to duty were important factors in clearing the Mediterranean shipping lanes for the safe passage of Allied convoys."

In August 1944, Wright transferred to the European theater where he served as Senior Staff Officer for the Naval Task Group Commander during the amphibious invasion of Southern France. He was awarded the Legion of Merit for:

"exceptionally meritorious conduct ... (He) directed the organization of escort units of convoys leaving the assault areas and the proper routing of ships and landing craft to the invasion beaches, efficiently scheduling and maintaining according to plan the precisely timed movements of an extremely large volume of shipping and skillfully coordinating the intricate operations of one hundred escort and patrol craft."

U.S.S. MISSOURI

From October 19 through November 18, 1944, as Atlantic Fleet Escort Commander, Wright was awarded a second Legion of Merit for:

"exceptionally meritorious conduct in the performance of outstanding services as Atlantic Fleet Escort Commander protecting trans-Atlantic convoys during WOrld War II. Undeterred by the hazards of enemy submarine-infested waters and adverse weather conditions, {he} skillfully directed the ships under his command in fulfilling the difficult assignment of transporting men and supplies to sustain the Allied war fronts in Europe."

On December 8, 1944 he reported for duty in the Bureau of Naval Personnel, Navy Department, in Washington DC serving there until July 1946 when he was ordered to the National War College for instruction, and he graduated in July 1947.

In July 1947, Wright was given command of Destroyer Squadron 13 (COMDESRON 13) and in July 1948 he reported for duty in the Office of the Chief of Naval Operations, Navy Department, serving for a year as Officer in Charge of the Plans and Policies Section, New Development and Operational Evaluation Branch, Fleet Operational Readiness Division, and a year and a half as Head of the New Development and Operational Evaluation Branch. He remained there until September 1950.

Following taking brief instruction at the Combat Information Center Schools in Boston and Philadelphia, Wright reported to the Office of the Deputy Chief of Naval Operations (Administration) In October,1950, where he remained until January 1951.

On March 2, 1951, Wright relieved Captain Irving Duke to take command of the *Missouri* towards the end of her deployment to Korea. *Missouri* continued gun strikes between March 14 and 19 at Kojo Wan, Songjin, Chaho, and Wonsan on the Korean east coast, aimed primarily at transportation complexes vital to the reinforcing and supplying of enemy forces in central Korea.

On March 28, 1951, *Missouri* was relieved of duty from the Far East and sailed for the United States and Norfolk, arriving there on April 27, 1951 where she again joined the Atlantic Fleet to train midshipmen and other prospective naval officers until October 18,

1951 when she entered Norfolk Naval Shipyard for an overhaul which would last until January 1952.

Upon entering the shipyard on October 18, Wright turned over command of the *Missouri* to Captain John Sylvester. Wright was awarded a second Bronze Star for his actions as captain, the citation reading:

"for meritorious service as Commander of a Task Group for gunfire support while operating with the US Naval Forces in action against the enemy in the Korean Theater during the period 2 to 28 March 1951."

The citation further stated:

"The Missouri served with credit and distinction as flagship of Commander Seventh Fleet, while participating in bombardment missions at Chongjim, Nanam, Chacho and Wonsan, on the eastern coast of Korea, effectively destroying enemy military, industrial and transportation targets in that area."

Detached from command of the *Missouri* in October 1951, he then joined the staff of Commander Cruiser Force, U. S. Atlantic Fleet, as Chief of Staff and Aide, and continued to serve in that capacity until October 1952, when he reported as Director of the Atomic Energy Division, Office of the Chief of Naval Operations, Washington DC., with a promotion to rear admiral on October 1, 1952.

In October 1955, Wright Commander Cruiser Division Five (CRUDIV 5), serving until December 1956, when he became Commander Military Sea Transportation Service, Western Pacific Area. He remained there until he was relieved from all active duty pending his retirement, effective March 1, 1958, with a promotion to Vice Admiral. His brother, Carlton H. Wright also retired as a vice admiral.

In 1926, Wright married Estelle Oliver of Falls Church, Virginia, and the couple retired to Coral Gables, Florida where he worked as in sales until 1962. He died in the Bethesda Naval Hospital in Bethesda, Maryland on August 7, 1987 at age 85 and was buried with full military honors at Arlington National Cemetery.

U.S.S. MISSOURI

Captain John Sylvester

John Sylvester was born in Wellston, Jackson County, Ohio on July 7, 1904, the oldest of three children born to John Edward and Ollie Richardson Sylvester. His grandfather was the city's first physician and his father was the editor and co-publisher of the Wellston Telegraph and he and his younger brother George, and sister, Janet grew up in Wellston, in a prosperous and prominent family.

Intelligent and a good student, Sylvester attended the University of Colorado before being appointed to the US Naval Academy from Colorado on June 13, 1922, less than a month before his eighteenth birthday. As a first classman, he was awarded the Thompson Prize for excellence in practical and theoretical navigation, the Class of 1871 sword for excellence in practical and theoretical gunnery, and the Gardener-Caskey Memorial Prize, a watch, for ranking first in his class, graduating on June 3, 1926 with a commission as an ensign in the US Navy.

Sylvester joined the Atlantic fleet, assigned to the USS *Concord* (CL-10), an Omaha-Class light cruiser that was commissioned in Philadelphia on November 3, 1923, operating as part of the Scouting Force.

U.S.S. MISSOURI

Concord participated in the Presidential Fleet Review taken by Calvin Coolidge on June 4, 1927. In May 1930, Sylvester, promoted to lieutenant (jg) reported aboard the USS *Manley* (DD-74) a Caldwell-class destroyer newly recommissioned as an experimental torpedo-firing ship, at Newport, Rhode Island. On August 19, 1930 she joined the Scouting Fleet in battle practice along the eastern seaboard and in the Caribbean. She performed similar duty on the coast of California out of San Diego during 1932.

In 1932, Sylvester reported to the Naval Postgraduate School at Annapolis for instruction and graduated with a Masters' degree in metallurgy from the Massachusetts Institute of Technology (MIT) in 1936.

In 1926, Sylvester had married Ruth Yarnell and now a decade later, in November 1936, he was assigned to the staff of his father-in-law, Admiral Harry E. Yarnell, Commander in Chief Asiatic Fleet (CINCAF), what after WWII became the Seventh Fleet, remaining with him the entire time of Yarnell's term.

LT. SYLVESTER (5th from Left) BESIDE ADMIRAL YARNELL

Serving as Yarnell's flag-lieutenant aboard the Northampton-class cruiser USS *Augusta* (CA-31), they operated out of the Philippines. Between November 5 and December 19, 1936, Augusta visited a succession of ports including Hong Kong, Singapore, Batavia, Bali, Makassar, Tawi Tawi and Tutu Bay, Dumanquilas Bay, Zamboanga, and Cebu, before she returned to Manila on December 19. Admiral Yarnell transferred his flag to USS *Isabel* on January 2, 1937, when *Augusta* entered Cavite Navy Yard for repairs and alterations.

With tensions with the Japanese increasing in the region, her alterations included the fitting of splinter protection around the machine gun positions at the foretop and atop the mainmast. Yarnell used *Isabel* as his flagship through March, rejoining *Augusta* at Manila on March 29, 1937.

Augusta sailed for Hong Kong on April 8th, arriving at the British Crown Colony the following day. Shifting his flag to *Isabel* for the trip to Canton, Yarnell returned to *Augusta* on April 13. *Augusta* sailed for China and arrived at Shanghai on April 24, mooring just upstream from the city. She remained at Shanghai until May 5, when she sailed for Nanking. The flagship remained at that Yangtze port from May 6 to May 9 before she got underway for Kiukiang, further up the Yangtze.

Shifting his flag to *Isabel*, visits to numerous Chinese ports followed including Hankow (Wuhan)and Ichang (Yichang), Chungking (Chongqing), after which Yarnell rejoined *Augusta* at Shanghai on June 2, 1937.

Augusta was conducting her usual training from Tsingtao when events in the region took a turn for the worse. Political relations between China and Japan had been strained over the steady and unrelenting Japanese encroachment into North China in the wake of the 1931 seizure of Manchuria. Chiang Kai-shek, China's leader, declared that China had been pushed too far, and on the night of July 7, 1937 Japanese and Chinese units exchanged gunfire near the ornate Marco Polo Bridge in the outskirts of Peking (now Beijing).

The incident quickly escalated into a state of hostilities in North China, with the Japanese taking Peking against little resistance by the end of July. Yarnell had considered cancelling a goodwill visit to the Soviet port of Vladivostok but was ordered to proceed.

U.S.S. MISSOURI

Admiral Yarnell sailed for Vladivostok in *Augusta* on July 24, accompanied by four destroyers. After passing through the edge of a typhoon, Augusta and her consorts reached that Soviet port on the 28th, and remained there until August 1, the first United States naval vessels to visit that port since the closing of the naval radio station there in 1922.

As Yarnell later wrote, *"both officers and men were lavishly entertained."*

Departing Vladivostok on August 1, *Augusta* and the four destroyers sailed for Chinese waters, the latter returning to their base at Chefoo and *Augusta* returning to Tsingtao, where Yarnell continued to receive intelligence on the situation in North China.

USS AUGUSTA (CA-31) CIRCA LATE 1930

Hostilities commenced within days after the death of a Japanese lieutenant and his driver near a Chinese airfield on August 9. With a considerable American presence in the International Settlement of Shanghai, Yarnell judged it best to sail there, arriving on the morning of August 13, 1937, to make it his base of operations.

Her passage slowed by a typhoon, *Augusta* reached her destination the following day, and sailed up the Huangpu River, passing many Japanese warships, principally light cruisers, and destroyers. Large American flags were then painted on top of *Augusta*'s three main battery gun turrets to identify her as neutral. On August 18 *Augusta* unmoored, moved further upstream, and moored off Shanghai and remained there, in a prominent position into January 1938, observing the Sino-Japanese hostilities at close range and showing the flag.

Initially, there was the problem of evacuating Americans from danger, but American merchant ships arrived at Shanghai, transporting passengers downstream to waiting steamships guarded by sailors from *Augusta*'s landing force. The flagship's Marine Detachment, meanwhile, went ashore to aid the 4th Marines in establishing defensive positions to keep hostilities out of the neutral enclaves.

On August 20, 1937, while the flagship's crew gathered on deck for the evening movies, a Chinese anti-aircraft shell landed among the sailors, killing Seaman 1st/Class F. J. Falgout and wounding 18 others. Ten days later Chinese planes bombed the American Dollar Line SS *President Hoover* off the mouth of the Huangpu, with one death and several wounded. American ships ceased calling at Shanghai as a result, and Admiral Yarnell's attempts to get a division of heavy cruisers to carry out the evacuation met resistance from President Franklin Delano Roosevelt.

Moored at Shanghai, *Augusta*'s officers and men could observe the war, offering the opportunity to size up the Japanese Navy and judge how well its ships and planes operated, an opportunity not lost on Yarnell, who sent insightful intelligence reports back to Washington, striving to alert the United States Navy to the character and capabilities of the Japanese Navy.

On December 12, 1937 Japanese naval planes sank the US gunboat USS *Panay* and three Standard Oil tankers north of Nanking, in the Yangtze River. Soon afterwards the ship's survivors arrived at Shanghai in *Panay*'s sister ship, USS *Oahu*, which moored alongside Augusta on the 19th. They spent Christmas with *Augusta*'s crew.

On January 6, 1938 *Augusta* departed Shanghai for the Philippines for her yearly overhaul. Yarnell however deemed his presence necessary to uphold American prestige in the Orient and remained in Shanghai with a token staff on board the Isabel. He rejoined *Augusta* upon her return to Shanghai on April 9, 1938.

Augusta operated in North China waters, between Tsingtao and Chinwangtao, for the remainder of the summer and through early

October. Sailing for Shanghai on October 10, the cruiser arrived at her destination two days later, and remained there through Christmas. She sailed again for the Philippines on December 27, 1938 and Yarnell remained in Shanghai.

Following her yearly navy yard overhaul, and training in Philippine waters, *Augusta* visited Siam, French Indochina, and Singapore before returning to Shanghai on April 30, 1939. On July 25, 1939 Admiral Thomas C. Hart relieved Admiral Yarnell as CINCAF, and Yarnell retired from active duty. Sylvester received a letter of commendation for his actions during the "Sino-Japanese hostilities".

From July 1939 until December 1941, Sylvester was assigned as Engineering and Research Officer at the Naval Torpedo Station, Naval War College at Newport, Rhode Island. In 1942 Sylvester went to Australia to interview submarine captains over the number of dud torpedoes during their attacks on Japanese vessels.

In 1943, Sylvester, now a commander, was assigned duty in the Pacific as executive officer aboard the Cleveland-class light cruiser USS *Columbia* (CL-56) newly commissioned in July 1942. Returning from Australia, *Columbia,* rejoined her division on September 24 off Vella LaVella, as patrols to intercept Japanese shipping continued. As Marines stormed ashore on Bougainville on November 1, Columbia's guns pounded targets on Buka and Bonis and in the Shortlands.

On the night of November 2, her force intercepted a Japanese group sailing to attack transports lying off Bougainville. In the resulting Battle of Empress Augusta Bay, *Columbia* joined in sinking the Japanese cruiser *Sendai* and destroyer *Hatsukaze* and turning the attackers back from their goal. She continued to support the Bougainville landings and bombard targets in the Solomon Islands through December.

Sylvester was awarded the Bronze Star with a combat "V" for his actions between October 30 and November 2, 1943. The citation states:

"Under heavy fire from hostile shore batteries and air raids, *Captain Sylvester rendered invaluable assistance to his Commanding Officer in the initial bombardment of Buka-Bonis and the first daylight attack on the Shortland Area. In addition to engaging a Japanese Task Force of superior fire power and sinking or damaging eight of the enemy's warships, Task Force THIRTY-NINE, of which the COLUMBIA was a unit, successfully fought off a deadly attack by sixty-seven hostile bombers, shooting down seventeen and repelling the others. Throughout these actions, Captain Sylvester's accurate evaluation of the tactical situation and his sound judgment under fire contributed to the protection of our beachhead at Empress Augusta Bay and to the successful establishment of our land and air forces on Bougainville Island."*

Late in 1944, Sylvester transferred to the staff of Commander Cruiser Division 4 (COMCRUDIV 4) for which he was awarded a Legion of Merit Medal *"for exceptionally meritorious conduct in the performance of outstanding services to the Government of the United States as Operations Officer aboard the U.S.S. COLUMBIA (CL-56), in Cruiser Division FOUR, during the Battle of Surigao Strait, on 25 October 1944."*

Sylvester finished the war serving on the staff of Rear Admiral W. L. Ainsworth, Commander Destroyers Pacific Fleet and in 1946, he took on the consecutive duties of Chief, Plans and Operations Division at the Armed Forces Staff College, Norfolk, Virginia and Director of Plans at the Naval War College, Newport Rhode Island.

From 1948-49, Sylvester commanded Destroyer Squadron 8 (DESRON 8), then from 1949-51, he served as Operations Officer, and later Chief of Staff to Commander 2nd Fleet whose area of responsibility included the Atlantic coast of South America and part of the west coast of Central America.

On October 18, 1951, Sylvester relieved Captain George T. Wright, to take command of the *Missouri* as it entered Norfolk Naval Shipyard for an overhaul, which lasted until January 30, 1952. Following winter and spring training out of Guantanamo Bay, *Missouri* made a port call at New York, then departed Norfolk on June 9, 1952 for a midshipman cruise. She returned to Norfolk on August 4 and entered Norfolk Naval Shipyard to prepare for a second tour in the Korean combat zone.

On September 4, 1952, Captain Warner R. Edsall, relieved Sylvester and on September 11, Missouri departed Hampton Roads for a second Korean deployment and Sylvester reported to Washington DC as special assistant to the Chief of the Bureau of Ordnance.

From January 1953 until November 1954, Sylvester served as special assistant to the Chief Armed Forces Special Weapons Project, at which time Sylvester was placed in command of Task Force 7.3 and Operation *Wigwam*. Sylvester was promoted to rear admiral on January 10, 1955.

Operation *Wigwam* was a single test of the Mark 90 "Betty" nuclear bomb conducted on May 14, 1955, occurring between Operation *Teapot* and Project 56. The test took place on May 14, 1955, about 500 miles southwest of San Diego, California and involved 6,800 personnel aboard 30 ships.

The test involved the underwater detonation of an atomic "device" to determine the vulnerability of submarines to a deeply detonated nuclear weapon, and to evaluate the feasibility of using such weapons in combat.

As the task force commander, Sylvester was responsible for the overall planning, development, and detonation of the test. Sylvester was embarked on the task force flagship USS *Mount McKinley*. *Wigwam* was the first atomic test in the deep ocean, and it remains to this day the only test conducted in water deeper than 1,000 ft. For his part in the operation, Sylvester was awarded a third Legion of Merit.

From September 1955 until May 1956, Sylvester commanded Amphibious Group 4 (PHIGRU 4), then from May 1956, he served as Deputy Chief of Staff for Operations on the Joint Staff of Admiral James L. Holloway, Jr., Commander in Chief Europe, with a promotion to vice-admiral on January 13, 1958.

In April 1958, Sylvester served as Commander Amphibious Force Pacific Fleet (COMPHIBFORPACFLT), later designated

Commander, Naval Surface Forces Pacific, COMNAVSURFPAC), responsible for all surface craft in the Pacific Fleet. On November 5, 1958, Sylvester hosted Fleet Admiral Chester W. Nimitz aboard his flagship USS *El Dorado* (AGC-11) during the joint army-navy landing exercise *Rocky Shoals* off San Simeon, California.

The exercise involved an amphibious assault on beaches near San Simeon on November 5. More than 13,000 troops embarked aboard a 40-ship task force of the U. S. Pacific Fleet were landed inland from the assault beaches in helicopters.

Exercise *Rocky Shoals* was a mock atomic war in which both the "Friendly Forces" and the "Aggressor" used tactical atomic weapons. Ships at sea and troops ashore maneuvered to present minimum targets for atomic weapons.

In June 1960, Sylvester was named Deputy Chief of Naval Operations for Logistics in Washington DC, where he remained until being placed on the retirement list on August 1, 1964 and retiring as a vice-admiral in 1965. He made his home after retirement in Washington DC.

Sylvester's first wife died in 1948, and he remarried Geraldine Clark. His son Charles, and two grandsons would also attend the Naval Academy and a second son, John Sylvester Jr. would have a career as a Foreign Service Officer.

Admiral John Sylvester died of pneumonia at the Georgetown University Hospital on July 26, 1990 at the age of 86. He was brought home to be buried at the Ridgewood Cemetery, Jackson County, Ohio.

U.S.S. MISSOURI

Captain Warner R. Edsall

Captain Warren Edsall brought a wealth of experience with him when he took command of the *Missouri* in September 1952. He'd commanded submarines and destroyers in war and had been awarded four Bronze Stars, all with combat V's. The United States was involved in the Korean War, and Edsall would steer the venerable old battleship through her second deployment to Korea.

Warren Ryerson Edsall was born in Hamburg, New Jersey on May 7, 1904, the second son of Robert Linn and Katherine Lawrence Edsall. His brother Rembert Taylor Edsall, ten years older, helped support the family after their father died in 1913.

After graduating South Philadelphia High School, and one year of college at the University of Pennsylvania, Edsall received an appointment to the US Naval Academy from the state of Pennsylvania, reporting on July 17, 1923. At Annapolis, Edsall played Tennis and was in the Musical Club. He graduated 49 in a class of 580 on June 2, 1927 and was commissioned an ensign in the US Navy. He was retained for aviation training at the academy in the summer of 1927.

Ens. Edsall reported aboard his first ship, the dreadnought battleship USS *Arkansas* (BB-33) at Philadelphia, and on September 5, 1927, *Arkansas* was present for ceremonies unveiling a memorial tablet honoring the French soldiers and sailors who died during the Yorktown campaign of 1781.

U.S.S. MISSOURI

Arkansas conducted training cruises in May 1928, when she took a crew of midshipmen into the Atlantic along the east coast, along with a trip down to Cuba. In June, she took part in a joint Army-Navy coast defense exercise as part of the hostile "attacking" fleet. In early 1929, Arkansas cruised in the Caribbean and near the Canal Zone. She returned to the United States in May 1929, for an overhaul in the New York Navy Yard.

Edsall, now a lieutenant (jg) transferred to the battleship USS *Wyoming* (BB-32). *Wyoming* was operated as part of Battleship Division 2 (BATDIV 2) Scouting Force as the flagship of Rear Admiral Wat T. Cluverius. She served until November 4, when she was withdrawn from front-line service and became the flagship of the Training Squadron, flying the flag of Rear Admiral Harley H. Christy. Thereafter, she conducted a training cruise to the Gulf of Mexico.

In 1930, Edsall attended to the Submarine School at New London, Connecticut, followed by assignment aboard the diesel submarine USS S-28 (SS-133). She departed the west coast for Hawaii in mid-February 1931, and on February 23 arrived at Pearl Harbor, Territory of Hawaii, where she operated for the next eight and one-half years.

From 1934-36, Edsall attended the Navy Postgraduate School at Annapolis, studying Naval Engineering, with a promotion to lieutenant on June 30, 1936, followed by a third year at the University of California, Berkeley where he earned a Masters' Degree in June 1937.

USS POMPANO (SS-181)

Edsall returned to Hawaii assigned as Engineering Officer of Submarine Division 8 (SUBDIV 8) attached to USS S-28 and USS S-24. In mid-1938, Edsall reported to Mare Island, California as executive officer aboard the USS *Pompano* (SS-181) a Porpoise-Class submarine commissioned on June 12, 1937, Lieutenant Commander Ralph E. Hanson in command. She operated off the West Coast of the United States, training her crew, and patrolling in a constant state of readiness. Edsall served as acting captain from January 31 until April 3, 1939, and Edsall left the ship on October 1, 1939. *Pompano* would be lost with all hands, on September 17,1943.

On May 31, 1940, Edsall took command of USS S-34 (SS-139) a submarine commissioned on July 12, 1922. He joined the ship in Manila and operated out of Pearl Harbor until April of 1941 when she returned to San Diego, California.

Edsall left *Pompano* on April 1, 1941 and reported to New London, Connecticut as Supervisor of Shipbuilding, Electric Boat Company. On July 1, 1941, he was promoted to lieutenant commander. He remained there until February 27, 1942 when he was assigned to the headquarters staff of Admiral Ernest King, Commander in Chief US Fleet in Washington DC.

As operations officer, Edsall was promoted to commander (temporary) on September 1, 1942 and he received two letters of commendation during this assignment, one from Admiral King *"for outstanding performance of duty as Assistant to the Fleet Operations Officer in Headquarters of the Commander in Chief, US Fleet, from February 27, 1942 to September 1, 1943"* and a second from the War Department: *"For meritorious service while attached to the Office of the Commander in Chief, U. S. Fleet, from February 28, 1942 to September 30, 1943".*

After attending the Fleet Sound School at Key West, Florida and the Naval Training Station at Norfolk, Virginia during October and November 1943, Edsall reported to the Federal Shipping and Drydock Company, Kearney, New Jersey, in charge of the pre-commissioning duties for the USS *Melvin* (DD-680).

The ship was named for Lieutenant (jg.) John T. Melvin who lost his life November 5, 1917 when his patrol boat, the USS *Alcedo*, was sunk by a German submarine in the war zone. The *Alcedo* was the first American war vessel to go down in World War I, and Lt. Melvin is officially recognized as the first American naval officer to die in the war.

Melvin was commissioned on November 24, 1943, with Commander Edsall in command and he would take them both into combat for the first time, and he would be awarded five Bronze Star Medals for his actions in the Pacific.

Following a shakedown cruise off the coast of Bermuda, *Melvin* sailed for the Pacific on February 1, 1944. Arriving at Pearl Harbor on March 4, she got underway for Majuro in the Marshall Islands five days later. For the next month, *Melvin* conducted antisubmarine patrols and participated in the blockade of enemy-held atolls in the Marshall Islands.

She returned to Pearl Harbor on May 2 to undergo intensive fire support training and on May 31, she departed for Saipan attached to Task Group 52.17 (TG-52.17).

Approaching that island on the night of June 13/14, she sank the Japanese submarine RO-36. A few hours later, while steaming off northern Saipan, she again attacked an enemy vessel, this time a merchantman, which burned brightly for a few hours before sinking.

For this action, Edsall was awarded the Bronze Star Medal with Combat V, the citation stating:

"in action against enemy Japanese forces in the Pacific War Area on June 16, 1944. When his ship obtained a night radar contact on a suspected enemy submarine, (he) immediately proceeded to close the hostile vessel and, after executing one attack which exhausted his supply of depth charges, assisted another destroyer in making a series of attacks. . . (contributing) materially to the probable destruction of the enemy craft as evidenced by a heavy underwater explosion one minute after the last depth charge pattern. . .floating debris, bubbling diesel oil and a large oil slick. . ."

Edsall would receive a Gold Star (2nd Award) for his Bronze Star for the same period, the citation stating "in action against enemy Japanese forces in Central Pacific Waters from June 13 to August 7, 1944. Contacting a large enemy merchant vessel, (he) *"daringly and relentlessly closed in to prevent the ship's escape and, in spite of intense return fire, scored numerous hits until the enemy's destruction was assured."*

For the next 23 days, *Melvin* provided counter-battery fire, conducted antisubmarine patrols, damaging an enemy submarine, served as call fire ship for Marines on the beach, escorted ships from Eniwetok, and participated in the bombardment of Tinian.

On July 8, *Melvin* sailed for Eniwetok, where on July 18, she sailed screening transports carrying troops to Guam, off the coast of which she screened transports and oilers from July 22 until August 7. After preparations at Guadalcanal, from September 8–21, she took part in the capture and occupation of the southern Palau Islands, then joined TG-33.19 for the unopposed occupation of Ulithi in the Caroline Islands.

After escorting LSTs to Hollandia, *Melvin* arrived at Manus Island to stage for the invasion of Leyte, Philippines. *Melvin* sailed for the Philippines on October 11, attached to Task Group 79.11 (TG-79.11), Edsall was not aboard, having turned over command of *Melvin* to Commander Barry Kennedy Atkins the previous day, October 10, 1944.

On November 22, 1944, Edsall assumed command of Destroyer Division 110 (DESDIV 110) and he would be awarded Gold Stars in lieu of two additional Bronze Star Medals. The first citation read *"For meritorious achievement as Commander Destroyer Division 110, aboard USS Laws, during operations. . .in the vicinity of Luzon, Formosa, the Ryukyus, French Indo China, the Japanese Empire and the Bonin Islands, and Volcanoes, from November 22, 1944 to March 5, 1945. . . (He) organized his ships to protect important heavy units of our Fleet from enemy submarine, aircraft and surface attacks…"*

The second citation read "For conspicuous achievement as Commander Destroyer Division 110 in action against enemy forces in the Japanese Homeland on February 15 and 17, 1945. With his division operating as an integral unitl of a destroyer scouting and patrol line which was at the time within 35 miles of the Japanese mainland, (he) expertly directed the ships under his command in destroying enemy aircraft, identifying, and homing our returning flights, rescuing personnel from damaged aircraft and providing early warnings of the approach of enemy forces…"

On March 20, 1945, Edsall was promoted to captain and assigned as Chief of Staff to Commander Cruiser Division 13

(COMCRUDIV 13). He was awarded a Gold Star in lieu of a fifth Bronze Star Medal:

"for meritorious achievement as Operations Officer on the staff of Commander Task Force 54 during operations against enemy Japanese forces in the vicinity of Okinawa from March 25 to May 5, 1945. By his professional skill and tireless energy, Captain Edsall rendered invaluable assistance to the Task Force commander in organizing, directing, and maneuvering his group in numerous combat missions while acting as gunfire and covering force during the assault and capture of Okinawa." He finished the war in that position, remaining until November 1945.

Assigned back at the Navy Department in January 1946, he served until April 1947 in the Office of the Chief of Naval Operations, then was designated Commander Destroyer Squadron 8, (COMDESRON 8) in the Atlantic Fleet, remaining until July 1948. For the next two years he served as Assistant Chief of Staff for Operations, on the Staff of Commander in Chief, Atlantic Fleet, serving Admiral William Blandy and then Admiral William M. Fechteler until July 1950.

From August 1950 through June 1951, Edsall attended the National War College, but with the ongoing hostilities in Korea, Edsall sought a combat command and on September 4, 1952, Edsall relieved Captain John Sylvester and took command of the *Missouri*.

Edsall sailed *Missouri* out of Hampton Roads on September 11, 1952 headed back to Korea for her second deployment and she arrived at Yokosuka on October 17. Vice Admiral Joseph J. Clark, commander of the 7th Fleet, brought his staff onboard on October, making the *Missouri* his flagship.

Her principal mission was to provide seagoing artillery support by bombarding enemy targets in the Chaho-Tanchon area, at Chongjin, in the Tanchon-Sonjin area, and at Chaho, Wonsan, Hamhung, and Hungnam during the period of October 25 through January 2, 1953. On November 20, the *Missouri* hosted a visit by South Korean President Syngman Rhee.

Missouri put into Incheon on January 5, 1953 and then sailed to Sasebo, Japan. General Mark W. Clark, Commander in Chief, U.N. Command, and Admiral Sir Guy Russell, Royal Navy Commander-in-Chief, Far East Fleet, visited the battleship on January 23. In the following weeks, *Missouri* resumed "Cobra" patrol along the east coast of Korea in support of the troops ashore.

The continuous bombardment of Wonsan, Tanehon, Hungnam, and Kojo resulted in the destruction of the enemy's main supply routes along the eastern seaboard of Korea. Her last bombardment mission was against the Kojo area on March 25. The following day, March 26, *Missouri* was passing through the submarine net at the harbor of Sasebo Naval Base in Japan for rearmament, when Edsall suffered a fatal heart attack His executive officer, Commander James R. North, would briefly command her until April 4, when he would be relieved by Captain Robert Brodie Jr.

USS EDSALL (DE-129)

Edsall left behind a wife, Margaret Harriman Edsall, a son, Robert Harriman, and a daughter, Margaret Katherine. His body was returned home and buried with full military honors at Arlington National Cemetery, Section 9, Site 6067. The destroyer escort USS *Edsall* (DE-129) was named in his honor.

U.S.S. MISSOURI

Commander James R. North

Commander James R. North would be one of three men to command the Missouri twice, once for only nine days, when as executive officer, he was acting captain upon the death of Captain Warner Edsall and a second time for four months prior to her first decommissioning.

James Robert North was born in Baltimore, Maryland on May 10, 1911 and after attending Gilman County School and the Baltimore Polytechnic Institute, he was appointed to the US Naval Academy from the state of Maryland on June 18, 1931. He was promoted to Midshipman-Ensign and graduated 67 in a class of 445 in June 1935 and was commissioned an ensign in the US Navy.

North reported aboard his first ship, the Tennessee-Class battleship USS *California* (BB-44) where he served from 1935 through 1941. The ship commissioned on August 10, 1921. North was aboard ship for Fleet Problem XVI, held from April 29 to June 10, 1935, the fleet conducted a series of maneuvers in the eastern Pacific, ranging from Alaskan waters down to Midway Island and Hawaii.

In mid-1937, *California* transferred to Battleship Division 2 (BATDIV 2), and on July 7, the ships of the division visited Hawaii, returning to *California* on August 22. *California* and her sister USS *Tennessee* transited the Panama Canal in early 1938 for a visit to Ponce,

Puerto Rico, which lasted from March 6 to 11. In 1939, North was promoted to lieutenant (jg).

In April and May, *California* participated in Fleet Problem XX, which was again held in the eastern Pacific. Following the conclusion of the maneuvers, Roosevelt ordered the Battle Fleet to remain in Hawaii permanently with the new forward deployment intended to deter Japanese aggression in the Pacific.

As tensions rose as a result of the war in Europe and the Second Sino-Japanese War in Asia, the Navy cancelled Fleet Problem XXII, which had been scheduled for 1941. Early that year, the ship underwent an overhaul at the Puget Sound Navy Yard that concluded on April 15, after which the ship made a visit to San Francisco.

In July 1941, North reported to the Naval Postgraduate School at Annapolis for instruction, taking a course on Ordnance, with a promotion to the rank of lieutenant on November 1, 1941. Graduating in December 1942, he reported to the Bureau of Ordnance in Washington DC in January 1943 where he remained until June.

In July 1943, North reported aboard the newly commissioned Essex-Class aircraft carrier USS *Monterey* (CVL-26). Future President Gerald R. Ford would also serve aboard the ship during World War II. After her shakedown cruise, she departed Philadelphia and after transiting the Panama Canal, she reached the Gilbert Islands on November 19, 1943, in time to secure Makin Island.

That November, North was assigned to the staff of Rear Admiral Marc "Pete" Mitscher, Commander Fast Carrier Task Force 38 (TF-38) and later Task Force 58 (TF-58) aboard his flagship, the Essex-Class aircraft carrier USS *Lexington* (CV-16). North was promoted to commander on March 1, 1944.

Nicknamed "The Blue Ghost" for erroneously being reported sunk by the Japanese four times, *Lexington* and North who served as gunnery officer and navigator, would participate in most of the major operations in the Pacific from 1943 through 1945 including Holandia, Truk, Saipan, Guam, the Battle of the Philippine Sea, Okinawa, the Battle of Leyte Gulf and air attacks on Japan. In her 21 months in combat, *Lexington's* planes destroyed 372 enemy aircraft in the air, and 475 more on the ground. She sank or destroyed 300,000 tons of enemy cargo and damaged an additional 600,000 tons. The ship's guns shot down 15 planes and assisted in downing five more.

For his performance in these assignments, North received a Letter of Commendation with Combat "V" and the Bronze Star Medal with "V" from Admiral Nimitz, Commander in Chief Pacific Fleet (CINCPACFLT). In June 1945, North returned to Washington, D.C. as Head of Analysis Sub-Section on the staff of Commander in Chief, United States Fleet, later COMINCH.

With the Japanese surrender in September 1945, North was assigned to the US Naval Mission to Peru on October 16, 1945, helping to advise the Peruvian Navy. In February 1948 he returned to the United States and in May 1948 North relieved Commander Paul Van Leunen Jr. to take command of the USS *Duncan* (DD-874), a Gearing-class destroyer commissioned February 25, 1945.

Just prior to North taking command, on March 1, 1948 *Duncan* suffered 2 killed and 14 injured in an explosion on board that caused extensive damage at the stern and the flooding of the after compartment from a hole at the water line."

After repairs at Long Beach, California, the destroyer rejoined the fleet for training until January 1949, when she again sailed for the western Pacific, this time for eight months. North turned command over to Commander Everett George Sanderson in May 1949.

In July 1949, he joined the staff of Commander, Air Forces, Pacific Fleet (COMAIRPAC) as Ships' Readiness Officer. In September 1951, he became an Associate Member of the Ships Characteristics Board in Office of the Chief of Naval Operations, Washington DC. On February 14, 1953, he reported as Executive Officer of *Missouri* (BB-63) at Sasebo, Japan.

Missouri resumed "Cobra" patrol with shore bombardment of enemy supply routes along the eastern coast of Korea, completing her final mission, the bombardment of the Kojo area on March 25. The following day, Captain Edsall suffered a fatal heart attack while conning her through the submarine net at Sasebo, and North assumed the duties of commanding officer until relieved by Captain Robert Brodie on April 4, 1953.

U.S.S. MISSOURI

North received a Letter of Commendation with Combat "V" from Commander Seventh Fleet for meritorious service as Executive Officer of *Missouri* from February 14 to March 26, 1953 and as Commanding Officer from March 26 to April 4, during combat operations in the Korean Theater. He again assumed command of *Missouri* on September 18, 1954 upon her arrival in Puget Sound Naval Shipyard for decommissioning on February 26, 1955.

North served as Commander Destroyer Division 52 (COMDESDIV 52) from April 1955 to May 1956. He was next assigned as Asst. Chief of Staff for Operations, Training and Plans to Commander Cruiser Destroyer Pacific (COMCRUDESPAC). In October 1958, he took command of the troopship USS *General H. W. Butner* (AP-113) in the Atlantic Fleet.

USS H. W. BUTNER (AP-113)

On October 14, 1959, North was relieved by Captain John Kelly Knapper, so that he could assume command of Destroyer Squadron 10 (COMDESRON 10), relieving Captain Phillip Hauck. In April 1961 North was assigned command of the Naval Ordnance Test Unit al the Atlantic Missile Test Range at Patrick Air Force Base, Florida.

In June 1963, North reported to Orleans France as the MSTS Representative for the Eastern Atlantic and Mediterranean Area, and then headquarters were moved to Frankfurt, Germany. The Military

Sea Transportation Service, (MSTS), later renamed the Military Sealift Command in 1970, was established in 1949 to consolidate shipment of military supplies from the four separate services used during World War II into a unified command.

Captain North retired from the Navy on July 1, 1965. In addition to the Bronze Star Medal and Commendation with "V" and one star, he was also entitled to wear the Presidential Unit Citation with two stars and the Navy Unit Commendation Ribbon.

Following retirement, North remained in Germany until his son completed his final two years at Army High School in Frankfurt. Originally married to Jeanette Keil of Beverly Hills with whom he had 4 children, she passed away in 1957 and he remarried in 1967 to Sybil Carmen North. They returned to Florida in May 1973 and settled in Stuart where in 1974 he became the first President of the Board of Director of Miles Grant, a yacht and country club development. Captain North died in Stuart, Florida on March 5, 1990 at the age of 78.

U.S.S. MISSOURI

Captain Robert Brodie

Captain Roger Brodie would fight battles during World War Two, seeing combat in the Atlantic, the Pacific, and the Mediterranean, but the battle that would result in the award of the Navy Cross would surprisingly be fought against the French.

Robert J. Brodie Jr. was born in the town of Owensboro, Kentucky on December 2, 1904, the older of two sons born to Dr. Robert and Georgina Lanauze Brodie. His younger brother, David Clarke, would be born in 1906. Brodie was admitted to the US Naval Academy on July 2, 1923, appointed from Kentucky.

He ranked 299 in a class of 579, and along with classmate and future Missouri captain Warren Edsall, he graduated on June 2, 1927 and was commissioned an ensign in the US Navy. He was retained at the academy for aviation training during the summer of 1927.

Brodie spent the first years of naval service aboard cruisers and destroyers before attending the Naval Postgraduate School at Annapolis as a lieutenant (jg) from 1934-1936. Promoted to lieutenant in 1937, he was assigned aboard the Lexington-Class aircraft carrier USS *Saratoga* (CV-3) in 1937.

Operating in the Pacific, *Saratoga* participated in a series of Fleet exercises. During Fleet Problem XVIII in 1937, *Saratoga*, under the command of naval aviation pioneer Captain, later full admiral, John H. Towers, covered an amphibious assault on Midway Atoll and was badly "damaged" by *Ranger*'s aircraft.

U.S.S. Missouri

The 1938 Fleet Problem again tested the defenses of Hawaii and, again, aircraft from *Saratoga* and her sister successfully attacked Pearl Harbor at dawn on 29 March. Later in the exercise, the two carriers successfully attacked San Francisco without being spotted by the defending fleet.

In 1938, Brodie transferred to the Mahan-Class destroyer USS *Cushing* (DD-376) as engineering officer. The *Cushing* was homeported at San Diego, and except for training at Pearl Harbor, conducted training exercises, tactics, and fleet problems along the west coast.

In 1940, Brodie reported to the newly created Navy Bureau of Ships, assigned to the Design Division, in Washington DC. The new bureau consolidated the functions of the Bureau of Construction and Repair (BUC&R) and the Bureau of Engineering (BUENG) and was responsible for supervising the design, construction, conversion, procurement, maintenance, and repair of ships and other craft for the Navy; managing shipyards, repair facilities, laboratories, and shore stations; developing specifications for fuels and lubricants; and conducting salvage operations.

Following the Japanese attack on Pearl Harbor and America's entry into the war, Brodie was promoted to lieutenant commander on December 8, 1941. On May 14, 1942, Brodie relieved Lt. John Norwood Ferguson Jr. to take command of the recommissioned USS *Dallas* (DD-199), a Clemson-Class destroyer originally commissioned on October 29, 1920.

From April 1 until October 3, 1942, *Dallas* escorted coastal shipping from New York and Norfolk, Virginia to Florida, Texas, Cuba, Bermuda, and other ports in the Caribbean. On October 25, *Dallas* departed Norfolk to rendezvous with Task Force 34 (TF-34) bound for the Operation *Torch*, the amphibious landings in French North Africa.

On November 8-9, U.S. Army troops, trying to take Port Lyautey, French Morocco and the airfield there, were bogged down by an unexpectedly tenacious resistance from 3,000 to 4,000 French troops and well-placed artillery. French aircraft periodically strafed the U.S. beachhead and engaged Navy aircraft in dogfights.

Subsequently, on November 10, the USS *Dallas* was given orders to execute a highly daring mission. to go ten miles up the narrow Sebou River in daylight. *Dallas* carried a U.S. Army Raider battalion and were given the mission to land them up the narrow, shallow, obstructed Sebou River to capture the airfield near Port Lyautey, French Morocco. The Fort Lyautey Airfield was needed as a base for U.S. planes to land, and ground troops were unable to capture the field from resisting Vichy French forces.

DD-199 USS Dallas

Earlier on November 8, *Dallas* had tried to break through the boom blocking the river mouth and had been driven off by intense French fire.

Now, before dawn on November 10, a net-cutting party on rubber boats, led by Ensign Mark Starkweather, succeeded in cutting the boom while under heavy French fire. Every one of Starkweather's men were wounded and Starkweather would receive a Navy Cross for his actions.

However, the dawn light would reveal that the breech was in shoal (shallow) water where *Dallas* couldn't go. Nevertheless, Brodie ordered *Dallas* ahead and she rammed and cut through the boom herself and proceeded up the shallow river against an ebb tide under heavy French fire, piloted by a Free French civilian, René Malevergne.

When the Germans had invaded France, Malevergne had wanted to fight but the Army had decided that at 50, he was too old. Retired from the French merchant marine, he lived quietly with his wife and two young sons in Mehdia, Morocco, where the Sebou River entered the Atlantic.

After France fell, he had joined the underground Resistance. His home became the last stop in Africa for the "underground railway" which helped young French and English airmen escape to England. During the day, Malevergne piloted cargo vessels up the muddy Sebou to inland Port-Lyautey. On specific nights, he rowed through crashing waves to deliver two or three airmen to a blacked-out ship waiting offshore.

Imprisoned by the Vichy French for anti-Nazi activity, Malevergne endured two months of questioning and solitary confinement, then was flown to France to stand trial. Somehow, he managed to convince the court that no one could guide a small boat through the mountainous surf off Mehdia. A few months later, the Germans shipped him to Casablanca on parole, where he was recruited by the OSS (Office of Strategic Services) forerunner of the CIA.

On November 10, despite Malevergne's knowledge of the river, *Dallas* ran aground multiple times in the tight and winding shallow river. In one case, a French near-miss lifted *Dallas'* stern out of the mud in which she was stuck, enabling her to resume progress.

Squeezing between scuttled French ships, obstructions that had been deliberately sunk to block the river, and passing through heavy French fire, *Dallas* continued upriver, returning fire along the way, taking out an unseen anti-tank gun that was holding up a column of U.S. tanks.

At one point, *Dallas* literally plowed a trench through the soft mud until she reached her destination at the airfield except for her bottom, virtually unscathed. *Dallas* embarked Army troops quickly captured the airfield. By 1030 that morning, U.S. Army Air Force P-40 fighters, flown off one of the U.S. escort carriers, were operating from Lyautey airfield. For his actions, Brodie would be awarded the Navy Cross.

Rene Malevergne was also awarded the Navy Cross, the first time in history, the Navy Cross has been awarded to a Civilian of a foreign nation. The citation read:

"Personally, taking the helm, Malavergne guided the destroyer through heavy seas, breaking over a bar at the mouth of the Sebou River, snapped a steel cable boom stretched across the river entrance and steamed into the channel. Though shore batteries, machine guns, and snipers on the banks kept the vessel under heavy fire, Malavergne threaded a tortuous way among the wrecks of merchant ships that had been scuttled in the channel, often literally ploughing through the mud of the shallow river bottom and landed the raider forces ten miles from an airfield that the raiders successfully captured." He would pilot a second ship later in the day.

On December 11, 1942, Brodie transferred command of *Dallas* to Commander Anthony Carroll Roessler and he travelled to Fore River, Massachusetts to take command on the newly commissioned USS *Ordronaux* (DD–617), a Benson-class destroyer, on February 13, 1943.

After her shakedown cruise, *Ordronaux* departed New York May 1, 1943 headed to Mers-El-Kebir, Algeria, escorting a convoy. Her first action against the enemy came on July 6, while at anchor at Bizerte Naval Base. Attacked by German planes, she helped shoot down several aircraft.

Ordronaux was assigned a squadron of PT (patrol torpedo) boats during Operation *Husky*, the invasion of Sicily on July 9-10, as part of Destroyer Division 32 (DESDIV 32) and she patrolled the harbor of Porto Empedocle, hoping to lure out German E boats and Italian MAS boats so that they could be destroyed. She also screened Allied ships from Axis submarines and rendered fire support for the invasion until July 21st.

Following the invasion, *Ordronaux* sailed back and forth across the Atlantic and through the Mediterranean Sea on convoy duty.

Brodie was detached from the *Ordronaux* on January 7, 1944 and he turned command over to Commander Jonathon W. Woodville. On June 22, 1944, Brodie, now a commander, traveled to Kearney, New Jersey to assume command of the newly commissioned Sumner-Class destroyer USS *Haynsworth* (DD-700).

After a shakedown cruise in the Caribbean, *Haynsworth* departed New York on September 20, 1944 escorting Queen Mary with Prime Minister Winston Churchill on board. Rendezvousing with British escorts on September 22, she returned to New York and sailed on September 26 via the Panama Canal Zone and San Pedro, departing on October 12 to arrive at Pearl Harbor on October 20.

On December 14, 1944, Brodie was relieved by Commander Stephen Noel Tackney, to take command of Destroyer Division 23 (DESDIV 23) which sailed on December 16 for Ulithi to join Vice Admiral John McCain's Fast Carrier Task Force 38 for the final assaults on the Japanese.

During the next three months, Brodie operated with the 3rd and 5th Fleets as part of the screen for the Fast Carrier Task Force, and Brodie was promoted to captain on March 20, 1945. Their primary mission was to conduct air strikes against strategic Japanese positions along the China coast, and Formosa, and to harass enemy shipping, and his ships provided support operations for the capture of Okinawa, followed by other operations off the main Japanese islands and in the Yellow Sea until the Japanese surrender on September 2, 1945.

Following the surrender, in mid-1946, Brodie served as Asst. Chief of Staff for personnel on the staff of Commodore A. J. Snackenberg, Commander of Joint Task Force One during Operation *Crossroads*, the first detonations of nuclear devices since the atomic bombing of Nagasaki on August 9, 1945. Held at the Bikini Atoll in the Marshall Islands, it was the largest peacetime military operation

Photo # 80-G-641298 Capt. Robt. Brodie takes command of USS Missouri

ever conducted by the United States, involving 41,963 men, 37 women, 242 ships, 156 airplanes, 4 television transmitters, 750 cameras, 5,000 pressure gauges, 25,000 radiation recorders, 204 goats, 200 pigs, 5,000 rats, and two atomic bombs.

During 1949-50, Brodie commanded Destroyer Squadron 11 (DESRON 11) in the Pacific. After duty at the Pentagon, Brodie assumed command of the *Missouri* at Yokosuka, Japan, relieving Commander North on April 4, 1953.

Missouri departed Yokosuka on April 7 and arrived at Norfolk on May 4 to become the flagship for Rear Admiral E. T. Woolridge, commander, Battleships-Cruisers, Atlantic Fleet, on May 14.

Missouri departed June 8 on a midshipman training cruise, returning to Norfolk on August 4, before being overhauled at the Norfolk Naval Shipyard from November 20, 1953 until April 2, 1954. Brodie was relieved by Captain Robert T. S. Keith a day earlier, on April 1.

For the next two years, Brodie commanded the naval section, Military Assistance Advisory Group (MAAG) in Taiwan, before returning to the US for his final assignment in Washington DC, assigned to the Navy Bureau of Personnel. He retired from active duty in 1957 and was advanced to the rank of rear admiral on the retired list.

Brodie served the next 14 years as a mathematics teacher at Bethesda-Chevy Chase High School, Montgomery County, Maryland. Brodie was married to Dixie Plummer Hill Brodie with whom he had two sons, retired Navy Lt. Cdr. Robert Brodie III (USNA Class of 1951) and David R. Brodie.

Admiral Brodie died on March 14, 1977 at the Collingswood Nursing Center in Rockville, Maryland after a long illness. He was buried with full military honors at Arlington National Cemetery, Arlington, Virginia.

U.S.S. Missouri

Captain Robert Keith

Captain Robert T. S. Keith's distinguished forty-year naval career would encompass both war, sending three subs to the bottom during combat in the Pacific, and peace, helping to negotiate the armistice at the end of the Korean War, as well as influencing future generations of naval leaders at the US Naval Academy.

Robert Taylor Scott Keith was born in Washington DC on May 19, 1905, the oldest of four children born to John Augustine Chilton and Mary Welby Scott Keith. His birth was followed by John Augustine Chilton Keith in 1907, Francis "Fanny" Carter Keith in 1909 and James Keith in 1911.

Keith grew up in Warrenton, Virginia and attended Stuyvesant School in Warrenton and the Severn School in Serverna Park, Maryland before being appointed to the US Naval Academy from Virginia on July 6, 1924. During his time at Annapolis, Keith played on the baseball team and was promoted to Midshipman 1st Class Petty Officer. He graduated 141 in a class of 173 on June 7, 1928 with a bachelor's degree in science and a commission as Ensign in the US Navy.

After being retained at the academy for aviation training in the summer of 1928, Keith reported aboard the Florida-Class battleship USS *Utah* (BB-31) in September 1928.

On November 21, shortly after Keith joined the ship, *Utah* departed Hampton Roads on a South American cruise, picking up

President-elect Herbert C. Hoover and his entourage in Montevideo, Uruguay and transported them to Rio de Janeiro Brazil in December, before transporting them home to the United States, arriving in Hampton Roads on January 6, 1929. According to the terms of the London Naval Treaty of 1930, *Utah* was to be converted into a radio-controlled target ship, and Keith was transferred to the Pennsylvania-Class battleship USS *Arizona* (BB-39) in October 1930.

In June 1929, *Arizona* entered the Norfolk Navy Yard for comprehensive modernization in 1929 and on March 19, 1931, even before *Arizona* was put through post-modernization sea trials, she hosted President Herbert Hoover for a brief vacation in the Caribbean. The President visited Puerto Rico and the Virgin Islands. Returning on March 29, Arizona conducted her sea trials at Rockland, Maine, before she was transferred to the West Coast in August with her sister USS *Pennsylvania* (BB-38)

In February 1932, *Arizona* participated in Grand Joint Exercise No. 4 in which carrier aircraft successfully attacked Pearl Harbor on Sunday morning, February 7. In March 1932, Keith left the Arizona to report aboard the USS *Overton* (DD-239) a recommissioned WW I Clemson-Class destroyer. Taken out of reserve in 1932, she was placed in rotating reserve commission, and served in that capacity until again decommissioned, in reserve, on November 20, 1937.

During one period between August 30 and September 13, 1932, *Overton* landed Marines in Nicaragua and her crew, including Keith, qualified for the Second Nicaraguan Campaign Medal. In May 1934, Keith left the *Overton* and reported aboard the ammunition ship USS *Nitro* (AE-2) as the communications officer. The *Nitro* operated primarily with the Battle Fleet in the Atlantic during fleet exercises. The ship was specially built to refrigerate and carry explosives and ammunition.

Additionally, *Nitro* was "configured to accommodate 10 officer and 250 enlisted passengers". She averaged three cruises yearly between the east and west coast by way of the Caribbean and Panama Canal.

In May 1935, Keith reported to the Naval Postgraduate School at Annapolis for instruction in the General Line course, and he graduated in June 1936, being promoted to lieutenant (jg) that same year, and he was assigned duty at the US Naval Observatory in Washington DC.

From May 1937 through June 1939, Keith served as aide and flag lieutenant on the staff of Rear Admiral W.T. Cluverius, Commander Base Force, Pacific aboard the flagship USS *Argonne* (AS-10). As Base Force flagship, she provided tender and repair services for minesweepers, tugs, and harbor craft, while maintaining the only major photographic laboratory for photo-triangulation of fleet gunnery exercises. Over the next seven years she operated principally out of San Pedro, California but followed the fleet to the waters of Hawaii or Panama to carry out her vital support duty.

USS AYLWIN (DD-355)

In June 1939, Keith was assigned as gunnery officer aboard the USS *Aylwin* (DD-355), a Farragut-Class destroyer commissioned March 1, 1935. The destroyer operated off southern California before entering the Mare Island Navy Yard on June 18, 1939 for repairs and alterations lasting until October 8. She got underway on the morning of October 11, bound once more for Hawaii.

Training intensified as war broke out in Europe following Germany's invasion of Poland on September 1, 1939 and the Navy formed a "Hawaiian Detachment" under Vice Admiral Adolphus

Andrew, based at Pearl Harbor, a step portending the basing of the entire Fleet there the following spring.

Aylwin arrived at Pearl Harbor on October 18, 1939 and, over the next few months, alternated periods in port at "Pearl" with varied exercises in the Hawaiian operating area. In the spring of 1940, *Aylwin* took part in Fleet Problem XXI, the last pre-war fleet problem. Indicative of the Fleet's security-mindedness at that time, *Aylwin* alternated with other destroyers conducting "security patrols" off the port of Honolulu and off Pearl Harbor's entrance, investigating all vessels sighted, including small fishing craft.

Detachments from the Fleet were rotated back to the west coast at intervals and *Aylwin* returned to the west coast during the summer of 1940, reaching San Diego on July 9 before shifting to the Mare Island Navy Yard on the 14th. She underwent repairs and alterations there until September 22, returning, via San Diego, to Pearl Harbor on October 21.

On February 7, 1941, she put to sea and, after rendezvousing with aircraft carrier USS *Enterprise* (CV-6) and sister destroyer USS *Farragut*, headed back to the west coast for a brief visit. They arrived at San Diego on February 13 but turned around again two days later and rejoined *Enterprise* which was ferrying a shipment of the latest Army fighter aircraft to Hawaii. The three ships reached Oahu on February 21.

On March 17, *Aylwin* left Pearl Harbor for off-shore patrol and exercises. Two days later, the ship conducted a two-hour night tactical exercise on a dark, moonless night. At its conclusion, all destroyers were directed to proceed to a rendezvous astern of the fleet's center. In the maneuvering, Farragut's bow sliced into *Aylwin's* port side at a 90-degree angle, causing extensive damage and nearly severing *Aylwin's* bow.

A fire immediately blazed up as high as *Aylwin's* masthead, illuminating the two ships and quickly spread aft through the wardroom and into the area occupied by the ship's officers' cabins. *Aylwin's* electrical installation burned with intense heat until controlled on the 20th. Fire parties from USS *Dale*, USS *Stack*, USS *Philadelphia*, and USS *Sterett* all contributed men to help contain the blaze; and a party from USS *Indianapolis* joined the one from *Philadelphia* in assessing the damage and making temporary repairs.

USS *Turkey* towed *Aylwin* back to Pearl Harbor for extensive repairs in drydock, and Keith, now a lieutenant, was ordered back to the naval academy in July 1941, assigned to the executive department. Headed by the Commandant of Midshipmen, the Executive Department is charged with interior discipline, drills, and all military and professional training at the academy. With the United States' entry into WW II following the Japanese attack on December 7, 1941, the navy expanded and on June 30, 1942, Keith was promoted to lieutenant commander, and three months later, on September 15, he was promoted to commander.

Between August and December 1943, Keith took instruction at the West Coast Sound School at San Diego, then on December 10, he relieved Lt. Commander Andrew J. Hill Jr. to take command of the USS *Nicholas* (DD-449) a Fletcher-Class destroyer commissioned June 4, 1942. Keith would be awarded three Legion of Merit Medals while in command of the *Nicolas* and see the most intense combat of his time at war.

On February 12, 1944 she resumed Central and South Pacific escort duties and for days later sank his first Japanese submarine. While operating east of the Marshall Islands on February 17, he made sonar contact with a submarine although whether Japanese submarine I-11 or a different sub has never been confirmed. As stated in the Legion of Merit citation:

"When his ship obtained radar contact on an enemy submarine while serving as a unit of the screening force destroyer, he initiated an immediate attack and skillfully maneuvered the Nicholas in the darkness to ensure the delivery of maximum gunfire…then conducting a series of depth charge attacks until sonar contact was lost, he received the assurance of its probable destruction of the submarine from floating deck gratings, bubbling diesel oil and a large slick visible for several days"

On April 5, along with Destroyer Squadron 21 (DESRON 21) she sailed to Milne Bay for temporary duty with the U.S. Seventh Fleet. On the 22nd, she covered the Aitape landings, on the north coast of Papua New Guinea, and until May 8 escorted resupply groups there and to Humboldt Bay. She then returned to the Solomons and the 3rd Fleet shelling Medina Plantation, New Ireland, on the 29th. Spending the first part of June on antisubmarine patrol, she again joined the 7th Fleet on the 14th, serving with Task Group 70.8 (TG-70.8) in the northern Solomons.

On August 15, she sailed to Manus Island to join Task Force 74 (TF-74) and operated along the New Guinea coast until the 27th. She then returned to Seeadler Harbor where she supported the Morotai operation from September 15–30.

On October 18, the *Nicholas,* now part of Task Group 78.7 (TG-78.7) escorted reinforcements to Leyte, arriving on the 24th. On the 25th and 26th, she patrolled off Dinagat Island and on the 27th set out again for Manus. On November 8 she sailed for Ulithi.

On November 12, 1944, *Nicholas*, which along with the destroyer USS *Taylor (*DD-468) was escorting the light cruiser USS *St. Louis* (CL-49) on a voyage from Ulithi Atoll to Kossol Roads at Palau picked up a surface contact on radar east of Palau at a range of 22,000 yards.

Nicholas closed the range and opened radar-directed gunfire with her 5-inch/127 mm guns, but the contact disappeared, suggesting that it was a submarine that had submerged. At around 10:30 pm, *Nicholas* acquired sonar contact on a submerged submarine, later identified as I-38, and she dropped a pattern of 18 depth charges but subsequently lost contact with the submarine. At about 12:30 on the morning of November 13, she regained contact and approached for an attack.

When her sonar operator reported that the submarine had made a last-minute hard turn to starboard, Keith ordered a hard to starboard, backing with her starboard engine as she did. The maneuver put her almost on top of the submarine, and she dropped a pattern of depth charges. A few minutes after the last depth charge detonated, a huge underwater explosion occurred, and with the sunrise, debris and human remains were sighted floating in the area. For this action, Keith was awarded a second Legion of Merit.

The Japanese submarine I-38 had been was armed with Kaiten torpedoes. "Kaiten" type human torpedoes were the first Japanese

"Special Attack" weapons, vehicles whose operational use involved the certain death of the crew, though their first successful employment followed that of the "Kamikaze" suicide aircraft by about a month. Proposals for human torpedoes were made in 1943 and were approved in early 1944, initially with provision for the survival of the operator. However, the extreme peril facing Japan after the loss of the Marianas in June 1944 led to acceptance of the pilot's death as an inevitable consequence of "Kaiten" use.

Keith was awarded a third Legion of Merit for "operations against the enemy Japanese in the Pacific over a period of 14 months…*maintain his ship at the highest standard of fighting efficiency*".

On February 6, 1945, he turned command of Nicholas over to Commander Dennis C. Lyndon and after attending East Coast Sound School at New London, Connecticut, he took command of the USS *Herbert J. Thomas* (DD-833) upon its commissioning at Bath, Maine on May 29, 1945.

The ship was named for Sgt. Herbert J. Thomas, a Marine killed while serving with the 3d Marine Division during the battle in the Solomon Islands on November 7, 1943. Discovering a gun emplacement difficult to approach, he carefully placed his men around him in strategic positions from which they were to charge after he had thrown a grenade into the emplacement.

When the grenade struck vines and fell back into the midst of his group, Sergeant Thomas deliberately flung himself upon it to smother the explosion, valiantly sacrificing his life for his comrades. For his heroic conduct he was awarded the Medal of Honor.

Keith's time in command of *Thomas* was brief, turning command over to Commander Walter James East Jr. on July 3, 1945, at which time he took command of first, Destroyer Division 17 (COMDESDIV 17) aboard the flagship USS *Turner* (DD-834) and later Destroyer Division 32 (COMDESDIV 32), aboard USS *Benner* (DD-807) and briefly commanding Destroyer Squadron 3 (COMDESRON 3) from February-March 1946.

U.S.S. MISSOURI

After shore assignment with the Bureau of Naval Personnel in Washington DC, Keith, promoted to captain on March 25, 1945, was assigned to command the Fleet Training Group and Underway Training Element at Pearl Harbor in June 1949.

In April 1950, Keith returned to the Naval Academy as the Secretary of the Academic Board and an aide to the Superintendent.

On April 1, 1954, Keith relieved Captain Robert Brodie as captain of the *Missouri* as she completed her overhaul at Norfolk Naval Shipyard on April 2, 1954. As the flagship of Rear Admiral R. E. Kirby, *Missouri* departed Norfolk on June 7 as flagship of the midshipman training cruise to Lisbon and Cherbourg.

During this voyage *Missouri* was joined by the other three battleships of her class, *New Jersey, Wisconsin*, and *Iowa*, the only time the four ships sailed together. She returned to Norfolk on August 3 and departed on August 23 for inactivation on the West Coast. After calls at Long Beach and San Francisco, *Missouri* arrived in Seattle on September 15. Three days later she entered Puget Sound Naval Shipyard.

On September 18, Keith turned command of Missouri over to Commander James North who commanded her until she was decommissioned on February 26, 1955, entering the Bremerton group, Pacific Reserve Fleet. It was North's second time in command.

From November 1954 through September 1956, Keith served as Commandant of Midshipmen at the Naval Academy, with a promotion to rear admiral on August 1, 1956.

From September, 1956 through August 1957, Commander Keith commanded the Destroyer Flotilla-Atlantic Fleet. In August 1957, Keith served as the commanding officer of the Subic Bay Naval

Base at Luzon in the Philippine Islands until March 1959 when he was named the Assistant Chief of Naval Operations for the Naval Reserve.

On March 9, 1960, Keith reported to San Diego as Commander Cruiser-Destroyer Force, US Fleet, for which he was awarded a fourth Legion of Merit Medal. In September 1961, Keith was appointed Senior Member to the United Nations Military Armistice Commission at Panmunjom, Korea, with a temporary promotion to vice-admiral on May 1, 1962. He was responsible for negotiating with representatives of Communist China and North Korea.

Keith took command of the US First Fleet, headquartered in San Diego, on May 5, 1962, but a heart attack in December 1963 forced his removal from active duty. He retired on May 27, 1964 after a forty-year career, and he was promoted to vice-admiral on the retired list. He retired to Virginia Beach and Coronado, California before settling in Falls Church, Virginia.

Keith married Eleanor Langhorne Hodgins on February 22, 1936 and the had twin sons, Captain Robert T.S. Keith Jr. USN (Ret.), USNA Class of 1958 and Langhorne, Lieutenant (jg) USNR.

Admiral Keith of congestive heart failure at home in Falls Church, Virginia on February 12, 1989 and he was buried at Warrenton Cemetery, Fauquier County, Virginia. His headstone reads *"He Fought the Good Fight. He finished the Course. He Kept the Faith."*

After her arrival at Bremerton, west of Seattle, *Missouri* was as a popular tourist attraction, logging about 250,000 visitors per year, who came to view the "surrender deck" where a bronze plaque memorialized the spot where Japan surrendered to the Allies, and the accompanying historical display that included copies of the surrender documents and photos.

Outside the gates, civilian businessmen made money selling *Missouri* souvenirs and other memorabilia. Nearly thirty years passed before *Missouri* returned to active duty. She would remain a popular tourist destination, and inactive for the next 32 years.

Captain Albert Kaiss

When Captain Albert Kaiss descended the gangplank of the USS *Missouri* on March 31, 1992, he became not only the last battleship sailor on active duty, but also the only man in US Naval History to both commission and decommission the same vessel. And the last commander to take her to war, for her third time.

Albert Lee Kaiss was born at Hagerstown, Maryland on January 10, 1940, the younger of two sons born to Frank and Autumn Lee Swain Kaiss.

He and his brother Thomas grew up in Hagerstown, and after graduating North Hagerstown High School in 1957, and earning a BS degree in Industrial Management from the University of Maryland in 1962, Kaiss enlisted in the US Navy.

After completing Naval Officer Candidate School at Newport, Rhode Island, Kaiss was commissioned an ensign and was assigned aboard the USS *Alamo* (LSD-33) a Thomaston-Class dock landing ship that was commissioned on August 24, 1956. A dock landing ship (also called landing ship, dock or LSD) is an amphibious warfare ship with a well dock to transport and launch landing craft and amphibious vehicles.

Kaiss joined the ship San Diego, following her return from an overhaul in San Francisco. She operated locally until October 16 when she got underway for the Far East with Amphibious Squadron 3. Enroute, several ships of the squadron were diverted to the Caribbean in response to the Cuban Missile Crisis, but *Alamo* was held in Hawaii on a standby basis. On November 17, she sailed to assist typhoon-stricken Guam, arriving with emergency supplies. After a two-day stop in Guam to unload supplies, the *Alamo* continued on to Subic Bay, in the Philippines. Local operations off San Miguel were held before the ship sailed to Hong Kong for the Christmas holidays.

Alamo made a port stop at Manila during the New Year's holiday in 1963 and then returned to Subic Bay. In January, she took part in the SEATO exercise Operation *Jungle Drum II*, off the coast of Thailand and then spent two days in Bangkok. Her next assignment took her to the flood-stricken island of Mindanao in the Philippines. The month of March was taken up by Operation *Silver Blade*, a large combined amphibious exercise off Taiwan. After three weeks of restricted availability at Subic Bay, *Alamo* sailed on April 20 for Yokosuka, Japan, before returning to San Diego on May 11.

In August 1963, Kaiss was assigned to the Dealey-Class destroyer escort USS *Lester* (DE-1022), named for Hospital Apprentice First Class Fred Faulkner Lester, a 19-year old hospital corpsman who was killed in action while assigned to a Marine Corps rifle company. He was posthumously awarded the Medal of Honor, for his actions on June 8, 1945, during the Battle of Okinawa.

Unhesitatingly crawling toward the casualty under a concentrated barrage from hostile machineguns, rifles, and grenades, Lester was wounded by enemy rifle fire, but stoically disregarded the mounting enemy fire and his own pain to pull the wounded man toward a covered position. Struck by enemy fire a second time before he reached cover, he succeeded in pulling his comrade to safety where, too seriously wounded himself to administer aid, he instructed two of his squad in applying medical treatment to the rescued marine.

Realizing that his own wounds were fatal, he staunchly refused medical attention for himself and coolly and expertly directed his men in the treatment of two other wounded marines, succumbing to his wounds shortly thereafter.

Operating in South American waters, practicing ASW maneuvers, Kaiss left the *Lester* in March 1964 to attend the US Naval Destroyer School at Newport, Rhode Island, graduating with Class #12 in September 1964, following which he was assigned to the Claud

Jones-Class destroyer escort USS *Charles Berry* (DE-1035) as the weapons and operations officer.

The *Berry* was named for Corporal Charles Berry, a Marine rifleman assigned to a machine-gun crew on Iwo Jima who, when an enemy grenade landed in the foxhole, unhesitatingly chose to sacrifice himself and immediately dived on the deadly missile, absorbing the shattering violence of the exploding grenade in his own body, saving the others and he was posthumously awarded the Medal of Honor.

Officers of the USS Berry (DD-1035) (Lt. Kaiss, bottom right)

The *Berry* was based out of Pearl Harbor, Hawaii operating in the West Pacific, with a deployment to Vietnam in August 1965. In June 1968, Kaiss transferred to the USS *Henry B. Wilson* (DDG-7) a Charles F. Adams-class guided missile armed destroyer, as weapons officer.

The *Wilson* was a new class of destroyers designed specifically to fire guided missiles. She was the first ship of her size to be side-launched and when launched was the largest warship ever constructed on the Great Lakes. Because of this, rather than being christened with the traditional champagne, she was christened with a bottle filled with water from the Great Lakes, the Saint Lawrence River, and the Atlantic Ocean.

Wilson deployed to Vietnam in 1968 and again in 1969-70, her third and fourth deployment to Vietnam, where she served as plane guard for carriers on Yankee Station in the Tonkin Gulf, participated

165

in Sea Dragon operations, patrolled on search and rescue duties, and carried out naval gunfire support missions. In June of her 1968 deployment, she was struck by enemy gunfire.

In June 1970, Kaiss reported to Washington DC, assigned to the Enlisted Personnel Detailing Section of the Navy Bureau of Personnel. From August 1972 through August 1973, he attended the Navy War College, Newport Rhode Island where he earned a master's degree in International Affairs from George Washington University.

In October 1973, Kaiss reported aboard the USS *McCandless* (FF-1024), a Knox-class frigate similar to the Brooke-class frigate but with an extended range and without a long-range missile system. In the 1970's the torpedo-carrying Gyrodyne QH-50 DASH (Drone Anti-Submarine Helicopter) system was replaced by a SH-2 *Seasprite* helicopter and the hangar and landing deck was enlarged.

During the early 70's most ships also replaced the 3-inch (76 mm) gun with an eight-cell BPDMS (Basic Point Defense Missile System) firing the RIM-7 *Sea Sparrow* missile, a short-range anti-aircraft and anti-missile weapon system, primarily intended for defense against anti-ship missiles.

McCandless's first deployment was a cruise to the Middle East that began in August 1973 and lasted through January of 1974. Following this initial cruise, *McCandless* adopted a regular schedule of deployments which took her to the waters of the North Atlantic, Mediterranean, Caribbean, and Persian Gulf.

In May 1975, Kaiss served ashore as executive officer of the Naval Recruiting District in Seattle, with a promotion to commander on October 1, 1977, then in April 7, 1978 he relieved Commander George E. Sullivan III and assumed command of his first ship, the Spruance-Class destroyer USS *Paul F. Foster* (DD-964) commissioned at Pascagoula, Mississippi on 21 February 1976.

USS PAUL F. FOSTER (DD-964)

Foster was the first Spruance-class destroyer assigned to the U.S. Pacific Fleet and became the first to fire a NATO *Sea Sparrow* missile. She was also the first to land a Boeing Vertol (Vertical Take-off and Landing) CH-46 *Sea Knight* helicopter on board her deck.

Departing San Diego, she became the first Spruance-class destroyer to deploy to the Western Pacific in March 1978. On May 11, 1980, Kaiss turned command of the *Foster* to Commander Theodore "Ted" Lockhart.

Following another tour of duty, as Surface Commander Detailer, at the Navy Bureau of Personnel in Washington DC from May 1980 until January 1983, Kaiss, now a captain, relieved Captain Timothy O'Keefe on January 21, 1983 to take command of the USS *William H. Standley* (CG-32), a Belknap-Class destroyer converted to a Ticonderoga-Class guided-missile cruiser in June 1975. *Standley* operated off the Pacific coast, homeported in San Diego. Kaiss turned command over to Captain Robert N. Giuffrenda on December 28, 1984.

Following 15 months preparing as prospective commanding officer of the soon to be recommissioned USS *Missouri*, Kaiss was involved in manning and reactivating the old warship after more than 30 years in mothballs. Responding to the Reagan Administration's program to build a 600-ship Navy, led by Secretary of the Navy John F. Lehman, *Missouri* was reactivated and towed by the salvage ship USS

167

U.S.S. MISSOURI

Beaufort to the Long Beach Naval Yard in the summer of 1984 to undergo modernization in advance of her scheduled recommissioning.

During her modernization, *Missouri* had her obsolete armament removed including the 20 mm and 40 mm anti-aircraft guns, and four of her ten 5-inch (127 mm) gun mounts.

The ship was upgraded with the most advanced weaponry available. Among the new weapons systems installed were four Mk 141 quad cell launchers for 16 RGM-84 *Harpoon* anti-ship missiles, eight Mk 143 Armored Box Launcher mounts for 32 BGM-109 *Tomahawk* cruise missiles, and a quartet of *Phalanx* Close-In Weapon System rotary cannon for defense against enemy anti-ship missiles and enemy aircraft. Also included were upgrades to her radar and fire control systems for her guns and missiles and improved electronic warfare capabilities.

**Gov. John Ashcroft, Mayor Diane Feinstein
and Captain Kaiss**

In San Francisco on May 10, 1986, in front of an audience of 10,000, Capt. Kaiss took command of the recommissioned *Missouri,* as the Navy Band played, and the crew ceremoniously ascended the gangplank. Among those in attendance besides Secretary Lehman included San Francisco Mayor Diane Feinstein, Missouri Governor John Ashcroft, US Senator Pete Wilson and Secretary of Defense Caspar Weinberger.

168

Shortly after taking command, Kaiss suffered a heart attack, and was relieved by Captain James A. Carney on June 20, 1986. But his navy career was far from over.

Captain James A. Carney

Captain James Carney would be one of the few *Missouri* commanding officers not a Naval Academy graduate, and one of the few captains to sail her into harm's way. And with 25 months at the helm, Carney earned the distinction of being her longest serving commander.

James Allen Carney was born at Fort Smith, Arkansas on September 6, 1939, the younger of two children born to James Ambrose and Nina Estelle Freeze Carney.

His father worked as Asst. Manager of The Arcade Department Store in Fort Smith and then was hired to manage Pfeifers Department Store in Hot Springs. Carney grew up in Hot Springs starting in the 5th grade at St. John's Elementary and then went on to graduate from Hot Springs High School in June 1957.

He attended Hendrix College in Conway, Arkansas, graduating with a double BA degree in Business and Economics in June 1961.

Carney then signed up for OCS in the US Navy, his preference over being drafted into the army, and went in with the intent to serve three years active duty, three years reserve, then get out and go to law school.

He reported to Officers Candidate School (OCS) at Newport Rhode Island in July 1961, as part of Class #56 and he was commissioned an ensign in the US Navy Reserve upon graduation on

U.S.S. MISSOURI

November 17, 1961.His first tour of duty was on the USS *Princeton* (LPH-5), an Essex-Class aircraft carrier converted to a helicopter assault ship in 1959.

Carney served as asst. personnel officer for 6 months, and then was promoted to assistant navigator, a position he served in for 2 ½ years. *Princeton* was deployed to the South China Sea for 6 months when he first joined her and participated in the escalating situation in Vietnam in 1962, the first of a number of future deployments.

In October 1961, *Princeton* rescued survivors of merchantmen serving in Pioneer Muse and Sheik, which ran aground on Daito Shima, and in April 1962 she delivered Marine Corps advisors and helicopters to Soc Trang in the Mekong Delta area of the Republic of South Viet Nam.

From September–November 1962, *Princeton* served as flagship of Joint Task Force 8 during the nuclear weapons test series Operation *Dominic*. Carney was promoted to Lieutenant (jg) on May 17, 1963 and left the ship in early July 1964. A month prior to his departure, the Bureau of Naval Personnel offered him the opportunity to "augment" to the Regular Navy, from the Reserves, and Carney accepted, making the decision to remain in the Navy for a full career.

In August 1964, Carney reported for 3 months of temporary duty aboard the Gearing-Class destroyer USS *Richard E. Kraus* (DD-849), which had been commissioned on May 23, 1946. The ship was named for PFC Richard Edward Kraus, killed in action on Peleliu Island on October 3, 1944. He received a posthumous Medal of Honor when, while trying to evacuate a wounded comrade from the frontlines, he threw himself on an enemy grenade saving the other members of his patrol.

After his temporary duty stint, Carney reported to the U. S. Navy's six-month Destroyer Department Head School in Newport, RI. Following graduation from Destroyer School, and qualified to serve as a Department Head in the areas of Operations, Weapons and Engineering, Carney reported in as the Weapons Officer in the USS *Robert K. Huntington* (DD-781) which had recently been equipped with RUR-5 ASROC (Anti-submarine rocket) missiles and the Gyrodyne QH-50 DASH (Drone Anti-Submarine Helicopter), a small drone helicopter built by Gyrodyne Company of America for use as a long-range anti-submarine weapon on ships. During this period, she operated off the east coast, in the Caribbean, and in the Mediterranean, and he left the ship in January 1967, with orders to report to Fleet Command Headquarters in Saigon, South Vietnam (via a 4-month training cycle in Coronado, CA).

From February through April 1967, Carney attended Counter-Insurgency (C.I.) School at Coronado, prior to being sent overseas for a one-year tour of duty in South Vietnam as a lone advisor to South Vietnamese Navy River Patrol Boats. He first served on an LSSL River Boat in the Mekong Delta, for about 6 months. He would recall:

"I was on my very first river patrol on the BASSAC River, when the LSSL (Landing Ship Support, Large) received an intense volley of gunfire from the shore line and I called in an Army helicopter for a counter-attack. The copter got there expeditiously, hovered about 50 feet directly above the LSSL, and immediately opened fire with a machine gun. The machine gunfire surprised me. It was my first battle action and my first thought was that WE were being fired at, and I almost called for another helo to assist.

Fortunately, I observed heavy foliage and palm trees falling to the ground and figured out what was happening."

Carney was then promoted to Operations Officer on the staff at Fleet Command Headquarters and lived in the McCarthy BOQ (a former hotel in downtown Saigon). He was present for the "TET Offensive" in which the North Vietnamese and Viet Cong invaded Saigon as well as the rest of South Vietnam. He was awarded a Bronze star with Combat "V" for his combat service in the Mekong Delta and during the TET Offensive.

Carney was transferred out of Vietnam exactly 365 days after arrival with orders to report to the NROTC unit at the University of Kansas as a Professor of Naval Science. He taught Naval Science at the University of Kansas from July 1968 until July 1971, teaching the freshman NROTC class at KU during his entire tour. In the process, he earned a master's degree in Public Administration from the university during his tenure. He was also promoted to Lieutenant Commander on August 1, 1969.

U.S.S. MISSOURI

Following his tour at KU, Carney attended the 10-month Command and Staff Course at the Naval War College beginning in August 1971. He graduated as a "Distinguished Graduate" in June 1972. Carney then received orders to OP-39 in OPNAV (Pentagon), as Anti-Air Warfare Training Coordinator, and later as Surface Warfare Officer (SWO) Coordinator in the Office, where he designed the first instruction on how to qualify as a SWO.

He returned to sea in July 1972 as the weapons officer aboard the Farragut-Class destroyer USS *Dewey* (DLG-14), the first U.S. Navy warship to be built from the keel up as a guided-missile destroyer.

Dewey's first commanding officer was Commander Elmo R. Zumwalt, Jr., who later served as the 19th 4-star Chief of Naval Operations. She was named in honor of George Dewey, the United States' only Admiral of the Navy.

The design of the Farragut-class destroyers was closer in size to a World War II cruiser rather than a destroyer and was originally referred to as a "frigate". *Dewey* had been decommissioned on November 21, 1969 and following an extensive conversion as part of the Navy's Anti-Air Warfare Modernization Program, *Dewey* was recommissioned on March 31, 1971 as a guided missile destroyer.

Returned to service in 1972, *Dewey* had West Pacific deployments supporting operations in Viet Nam. In later operations in the Atlantic (late 1973/early 1974), *Dewey* was involved in the Yom Kippur Conflict and participated in a Radar picket at Crete.

In October 1975, Carney was assigned as the Executive Officer of the Knox-Class frigate USS *Jesse L. Brown* (FF-1089).

Commissioned on February 17, 1973, the ship was named for Ensign Jesse Leroy Brown, the navy's first African-American aviator, who was killed in action during the Korean War.

Brown departed her home port at Charleston, SC, on August 19, 1975 in company with USS *Valdez* (FF-1096), on her second extended deployment to the Mediterranean and the Middle East. The frigates proceeded together to Port Said, Egypt, arriving on September 4 and the next day transited the Suez Canal and steamed to Djibouti, French Territory of the Afars and Issas. On September 12, the frigates departed Djibouti and conducted exercises with units from the French navy.

Brown detached from the group later that day and sailed for Iran. The ship spent a week at Bandar Abbas, September 21–28, in conjunction with a three-day exercise with Faramarz, Palang, and Milanian of the Royal Iranian Navy as well as Valdez. *Brown* called at Karachi, Pakistan, from November 5–10 prior to exercises with the Pakistani Navy from the 10th–14th. For the next two weeks, the frigate participated in Exercise Midlink 75 from November 15–29 and then returned to Manama, Bahrain. The ship operated in the Persian Gulf until December 17 and then spent the holiday season at Manama.

Brown departed on January 3, 1976 with members of the Royal Saudi Navy embarked. After a brief stop to refuel at Bandar Abbas on the 12th, the ship called at Muscat, Oman where she exchanged 21-gun salutes with the Omani Navy. After departing Muscat on the 17th, the frigate completed an exercise with the Omanis and then made a return visit to Djibouti, January 21–23 and a fuel stop at Port Sudan, Sudan on the 27th.

At Jidda, Saudi Arabia, on January 28–29, *Brown* disembarked the party from the Royal Saudi Navy and completed turnover with USS *Garcia* (FF-1040). Arriving at Port Suez on January 30, the ship transited the Suez Canal the next day and headed west across the Mediterranean to Rota. On February 11, 1976, the frigate arrived at Brest, France, for a special Bicentennial visit.

On February 14, 1778, while the Americans were engaged in their war for independence from Britain, the French Admiral Toussaint-Guillaume Picquet de la Motte extended the first official recognition of the American flag by a foreign power with a gun salute to the Continental Navy sloop *Ranger*, commanded by Capt. John Paul Jones, at Quiberon Bay, France.

U.S.S. MISSOURI

Commemorating the anniversary of that historic event, at the conclusion of the port call on February 14, *Brown* exchanged gun salutes with the French destroyer *Dupetit-Thouars* (D.625). During the frigate's Atlantic transit, she stopped for fuel at Ponta Delgada in the Azores and at Port Royal

Bay, Bermuda before returning home to Charleston on February 25 to begin post-deployment leave and upkeep.

The *Brown* got underway again on June 4, 1976 to conduct midshipman training at Newport, Rhode Island, then sailed in to Boston, Mass., on June 16 to take part in that city's Bicentennial celebration. She returned to Charleston on June 28 and prepared for her Board of Inspection and Survey inspection, which took place in mid-July. On July 26, ten midshipmen embarked for training.

Over the next two months, the ship conducted numerous exercises. On October 4, 1976, *Brown* was again assigned as part of the Naval On-Call Force-Mediterranean (NAVOCFORMED), and set out for the Mediterranean, visiting Tangier, Morocco, Gaeta, Italy, and La Spezia, Italy.

On October 25, *Brown* got underway with the other units of the NATO force; *Mohawk* (F.125) and *Tidereach* (A.96) of Britain, *Berk* (D.358) from Turkey, and Italy's *Indomito* (D.559).

Over the next month, the ships visited Marseilles, France; Catania and Taranto, Italy; and Izmit, Turkey, before NAVOCFORMED was deactivated. *Brown* then arrived at Athens, Greece, on November 25.

During the first two weeks of December, the frigate completed training evolutions at Augusta Bay, Sicily, and Souda Bay, Crete. She called at Izmir, Turkey, and then on December 20 put in to Athens for upkeep at Elefsis Shipyard. Resuming operations for the Sixth Fleet on 10 January 1977, *Brown* proceeded to Kithira anchorage off the coast of Greece to rendezvous with Task Group 60 for operations.

On January 20, the frigate participated in missile and gunnery exercises on the NATO Missile Firing Installation near Souda Bay.

At the end of January, the ship engaged in plane guard operations and ASW exercises and made port calls at San Remo, Italy, and Palma de Mallorca, Spain, in February.

Following a four-day port visit at Gaeta, Italy, in early March, the frigate completed coordinated submarine operations with the nuclear-powered USS *Sunfish* (SSN-649).

She then spent a week at Livorno, Italy in March and took part in National Week XXII as part of the Blue Force Amphibious Group with the USS *Guam* (LPH-9), USS *Mount Baker* (AE-34) USS *Harlan County* (LST-1196), USS *Fort Snelling* (LSD-30), and the *Valdez* from March 19–25 and the post-exercise critique at Augusta Bay on the 26th.

The *Brown* called at Valencia, Spain then steamed to Lisbon, Portugal, arriving on April 8. On the 12th, the ship held turnover with the USS *Tattnall* (DDG-19) and departed for home, reaching Charleston on April 21. Carney was promoted to commander on April 1, 1977 and departed the ship, assigned to the staff of Commander Naval Surface Force, US Pacific Fleet (COMNAVSURFPAC) at San Diego, to serve as the Force ASW Officer.

USS LEFTWICH (DD-984)

In March 1979, Carney was named pre-commissioning commanding officer (PCO) for the USS *Leftwich* (DD-984), a Spruance-Class destroyer named for Lieutenant Colonel William G.

Leftwich, Jr., commander of the Marine 1st Reconnaissance Battalion, who was killed in action during Operation Imperial Lake in Quảng Nam Province South Vietnam on November 18, 1970 in a helicopter crash during the extraction of one of his reconnaissance teams.

The *Leftwich* was commissioned on August 25, 1979 with Carney as her first commanding officer. The Commissioning speaker was the Chief of Naval Operations, Admiral Thomas B. Hayward, a classmate of Leftwich at the US Naval Academy. Also in attendance at the Commissioning was H. Ross Perot, also a classmate of Lieutenant Colonel Leftwich. Both of Colonel Leftwich's sons and his widow attended the commissioning as well.

Leftwich sailed from Pascagoula, MS the morning following her commissioning on August 26, heading via the Panama Canal for her homeport, Naval Station San Diego, from which she operated until March 1985. Following her arrival in San Diego, *Leftwich* conducted "Shakedown" training under the guidance of Fleet Training Group, Pacific, in the San Diego Operations Area.

In January 1980, *Leftwich* returned to Litton Industries at Pascagoula, MS, for Warranty repairs and a Post-Shakedown Availability, which included the installation of the NATO *Sea Sparrow* system and *Harpoon* missile systems. He was promoted to the rank of Captain on June 1, 1982.

On August 14, 1982, Carney turned command over to Commander James Lawrence Burke and he reported to Washington DC, back at the Pentagon, from October 1982 through February 1985 as Program Director of the Aegis Shipbuilding and Weapons Development Program, managing the building of 27 Aegis cruisers and 61 Aegis destroyers.

Later, he served as executive assistant to the Director-Research, Development, Test and Evaluation (OP-98) from February through October 1985. From November 1985 until June 1986, Carney attended various schools, including 4 weeks of Commander Tactical Training in November and the AEGIS Combat System Officer, or AEGIS PCO/PXO Course, for 4 weeks in February 1986.

Carney's initial set of orders included PCO and commissioning CO of the USS *Thomas S. Gates* (CG-51), an Aegis cruiser; however, the original recommissioning CO of USS *Missouri* (BB-63) Captain Al Kaiss, developed a heart valve problem, and was medically disqualified to be the CO and Captain Carney received a call from the head of the Surface Navy (OP-03) asking if he would be interested in becoming the CO of the *Missouri* instead of the *Gates*

Captain Carney was given command of the *Missouri* on June 20, 1986, and soon after the Navy ordered *Missouri* to depart her home port, Long Beach, CA, for an around-the-world cruise. Visiting Pearl Harbor, Hawaii, Sydney, Hobart, and Perth, Australia, Diego Garcia, the Suez Canal; Istanbul, Turkey, Naples, Italy, Rota, Spain, Lisbon, Portugal and the Panama Canal. *Missouri* became the first American battleship to circumnavigate the globe since Theodore Roosevelt's "Great White Fleet" 80 years earlier, a fleet that included the first battleship USS *Missouri* (BB-11). She arrived back home at Long Beach on December 19.

Following local operations and battle group training in early 1987, *Missouri* was outfitted with 40 mm grenade launchers and 25 mm chain guns and departed for the Persian Gulf on July 25, 1987 to take part in Operation *Earnest Will*, (July 24, 1987 – September 26, 1988) protecting Kuwaiti-owned tankers from Iranian attacks during the Iran–Iraq War. It was the largest naval convoy operation since World War II. These smaller-caliber weapons were installed due to the threat of Iranian Boghammar fast attack craft operating in the Persian Gulf.

Missouri departed on a six-month deployment to the Indian Ocean and North Arabian Sea, spending more than 100 continuous days at sea in a hot, tense environment. She stopped at Subic Bay in the Philippines before conducting an exercise with Singapore Navy units in mid-August. Transiting the Strait of Malacca on August 25-26, Missouri sailed to the north Arabian Sea for operations with the USS *Ranger* (CV-61) Battle Group Echo.

As the centerpiece for Battlegroup Echo, *Missouri* escorted tanker convoys through the Strait of Hormuz, keeping her fire control system trained on land-based Iranian Silkworm missile launchers. The *Missouri* supported tanker convoy operations in the region for the next three months, pausing only for short port visits for maintenance at Muscat, Oman.

U.S.S. MISSOURI

Carney recalled: *"Upon arrival in the Indian Ocean, MISSOURI's first task was to reopen the Strait of Hormuz to permit a large convoy of international oil tankers to proceed into the Persian Gulf, which had been closed after Iran's distribution of numerous mines in and around the Strait. The SS Bridgeton hit one of the mines while exiting the Strait which closed the waterway for an extended period of time.*

When Missouri entered the Strait, she encountered a medium-sized Iranian craft which was in the middle of the waterway, apparently making certain no oil tankers would attempt to make it through.

We were escorted by an Aegis cruiser for protection against Iranian anti-ship cruise missiles and we had all our 16-inch guns pointed at potential targets on the shore. The Iranian craft departed the Strait at top speed and was never seen again.

The entire convoy of oil tankers then passed through the Strait of Hormuz with no difficulty. The Missouri Battle Group spent close to nine months in the area, at one point operating more than 100 continuous days at sea in a hot, tense environment."

After turnover to a different battle group on November 24, *Missouri* steamed home via Diego Garcia where the crew was surprised by singer Wayne Newton in a concert held on the island. She then proceeded to Fremantle, Sydney and Pearl Harbor, before returning to Long Beach on January 19, 1988. In early March, *Missouri* visited Vancouver, British Columbia, then shifted south to San Diego for gunnery, cruise missile and other war-at-sea evolutions. The crew also conducted the first *Tomahawk* cruise missile launch from the battleship on May 25.

Missouri then participated in Rim Pac'88, a large 40-ship multi-national exercise in Hawaiian waters in July, before Carney turned command of *Missouri* over to Captain John J. Chernesky on July 6, 1988.

Carney retired shortly afterward to return to home to be present during his oldest son's entry into the University of Arkansas, followed by his entry into law school. His youngest son then attended the U of A where he earned both a bachelor's degree and a master's degree. Carney's retirement officially occurred on August 1, 1988, following a 27-year naval career. His awards include two Legions of

Merit, a Bronze Star Medal with Combat V, the Combat Action Ribbon, and numerous other awards.

Carney married Betty Kate Brown on July 25, 1964 and they have two sons, James Allen Jr. born in August 1969 and Peter Logan, born in December 1972. After retiring, Carney formed his own corporation (Carney and Associates), consulting on national defense issues. He currently lives in Hot Springs, Arkansas.

U.S.S. MISSOURI

Captain John J. Cherneskey

Captain Cherneskey's time in command of the *Missouri* was relatively uneventful and would cap a 23-year naval career that primarily involved service aboard submarines, earning the coveted dolphin badge, yet his commands would be aboard a frigate and battleship.

John Joseph Cherneskey Jr. was born in the town of Hampton, New Hampshire on July 6, 1944 to John Joseph Sr. and Mary Jane Milewski Cherneskey.

He and his brother Thomas were raised in Hampton and were active in church and the community. After graduating high school in 1963, Cherneskey attended the University of Miami in Ohio, graduating in June 1967 with a BS degree in Nautical Science and Mathematics.

After enlisting in the navy, Cherneskey attended Officer Candidate School at Newport, Rhode Island and was commissioned an ensign in the US Navy Reserve. His first assignment was to Submarine School at New London, Connecticut enrolled in the Officers Basic Course.

From the end of 1967 until 1969, Cherneskey served as the Communications Officer and Asst. Engineer aboard the submarine USS *Tench* (SS-417), commissioned in October 1944. Utilized primarily as a training ship for the submarine school, *Tench* broke that routine for a four-month cruise with the Sixth Fleet. Upon completion of that deployment, she returned once again to her New London-based training operations which occupied the submarine for the remainder of her active career.

During the late summer and early fall of 1968, *Tench* took part in a NATO exercise, Operation "*Silvertower,*" in the eastern Atlantic. During that assignment, she visited ports in the United Kingdom, Germany, and Portugal.

The submarine returned to New London on November 4, 1968 and began her final 19 months of active service. Near the end of her career, she was given hull classification symbol AGSS-417 (general auxiliary submarine). Cherneskey, promoted to lieutenant (jg), left the ship in 1969, assigned to the Tang-Class submarine USS *Wahoo* (SS-565) as Communications Officer and Engineering Officer.

The *Wahoo*, commissioned May 30, 1952, departed her homeport of Pearl Harbor on February 11, 1969, on her way to the Far East for the eighth deployment. That deployment brought only a very brief tour in the Vietnam combat zone. Otherwise, she conducted a normal peacetime deployment visiting Oriental ports and participating in Seventh Fleet training exercises.

She returned to Pearl Harbor on August 14 and took up her usual training routine in the Hawaiian Islands. Her ninth tour of duty in the western Pacific began on April 1, 1970. During the last week of the month, she again cruised briefly in the combat zone off Vietnam but, as with the previous deployment, she spent the remainder engaged in a normal Seventh Fleet schedule of operations. She returned to Pearl Harbor on October 21 and began an overhaul which was completed on June 1, 1971.

On the same day that she completed her overhaul, Wahoo departed Pearl Harbor and shaped a course for her new home port, San Diego, California, visiting Portland, Oregon, and Vancouver, British Columbia before arriving at San Diego on June 26, 1971 and Cherneskey, now promoted to lieutenant, left the ship.

Later in 1971, Cherneskey was assigned as Flag Lieutenant and aide to Rear Admiral Paul L. Lacy, Jr., the last WW2 submarine skipper in the job, and later Rear Admiral Frank D. McMullen, Commander Submarine Pacific (COMSUBPAC) and Commander Naval Submarine Force (COMNAVSUBFOR), remaining in that post until 1973.

CAPTAIN JOHN J. CHERNESKEY

From 1973-75, Cherneskey, now a lieutenant-commander, was assigned as Executive Officer and Weapons Officer aboard the Barbel-Class diesel-electric submarine USS *Blueback* (SS-581). In September 1973, she deployed to the Western Pacific, participating in the 1974 UNITAS Exercise. UNITAS is a longstanding, multinational maritime exercise conducted annually in Latin America and the Caribbean to enhance security cooperation and improve coalition operations.

In 1975, Cherneskey reported aboard the Barbel-Class submarine USS *Bonefish* (SS-582) as Navigator, Operations Officer and Executive Officer. *Bonefish*, homeported at Pearl Harbor, operated locally until December 6, 1975, when she departed Oahu bound for the Orient. During that tour of duty, she participated in exercises with units of the Korean and Taiwanese navies as well as with elements of the Japanese Maritime Self-Defense Force. She concluded 7th Fleet assignments on April 25, 1976 when she departed Subic Bay and arrived back in Pearl Harbor on May 15.

After a four-week stand-down and a brief period of operations, *Bonefish* entered the Pearl Harbor Naval Shipyard on July 26. The repairs and modifications took nearly a year to complete. She emerged from the shipyard on June 25, 1977 and Chernesky reported to Washington DC for shore duty.

From 1977-79, Cherneskey served first at the Bureau of Naval Personnel (BUPERS) at the Career Planning Branch, then working on Officer Retention in the Office of the Chief of Naval Operations. During this time, he completed postgraduate work in management at George Washington University, and was promoted to full commander.

U.S.S. Missouri

From 1979 to 1981, Cherneskey served as the executive officer aboard the USS *Dale* (CG-19), a Leahy-class cruiser commissioned on November 23, 1963. *Dale* operated in the North Atlantic, Mediterranean and Indian Ocean. She served as the flagship for the Commander Striking Force Atlantic Fleet for the NATO exercise "Ocean Safari."

In January and February 1980, *Dale* participated in the Atlantic Fleet Readiness Exercise "READEX 1-80", then deployed to the Mediterranean Sea in March 1980 and, as a unit of the Sixth Fleet, serving as the flagship of Commander-Destroyer Group Eight.

A highlight of this deployment was entering the Black Sea to visit Constanța, Romania. *Dale* returned to Mayport in August 1980. The remainder of the year included two trips to the Caribbean for carrier support operations and participations in "COMPUTEX/ASWEX 1-81."

Dale entered the Charleston Naval Shipyard in March 1981 to begin a Baseline Overhaul to update the ship's combat weapons systems and overhaul major engineering equipment. During the overhaul, on July 23, 1981, Cherneskey left the ship and relieved Captain Robert W. Sherer to take command of the Knox-class frigate USS *Patterson* (FF-1061).

After sailing east into the Mediterranean in October 1980, *Patterson* toured the Persian Gulf during the last months of that year and the first month of 1981. A fifth Sixth Fleet cruise followed from late in 1981 into 1982, with Red Sea operations at the end of the deployment. The frigate earned a Meritorious Unit Commendation for her activities during this time. In June 1983 Patterson was assigned to the Naval Reserve Force, and on July 9, Cherneskey turned command of *Patterson* over to Commander John Richard Heufelder.

Cherneskey reported to Avondale Shipyard near New Orleans, Louisiana as recommissioning XO for the battleship USS *Iowa* (BB-61), assisting in the refitting and equipment modernization in advance of her recommissioning. *Iowa* was then towed to Ingalls Shipbuilding, Pascagoula, Mississippi, where over several months she was upgraded with the most advanced weaponry available.

Among the new weapons systems installed were four MK 141 quad cell launchers for 16 AGM-84 *Harpoon* anti-ship missiles, eight Armored Box Launcher mounts for 32 BGM-109 *Tomahawk* missiles, and a quartet of *Phalanx* Close-in weapon system Gatling guns for defense against enemy anti-ship missiles and enemy aircraft.

USS IOWA (BB-61) IN WAR CAMOFLAUGE

Cherneskey was promoted to captain on March 13, 1984, and *Iowa* was formally recommissioned on April 28, 1984, ahead of schedule, within her budget at a cost of $500 million, and under the command of Captain Gerald E. Gneckow. From April to August 1984, *Iowa* underwent refresher training and naval gunfire support qualifications at Guantanamo Bay, Cuba, and the Puerto Rican Operating area.

After a short period in her new home port of Norfolk, VA she spent the two periods of time during the rest of 1984 and early 1985 conduction "presence" operations shakedown in the area around Central America. During this time, she transited the Panama Canal to operate off the west coast of Central America while also conducting humanitarian operations, including in El Salvador, Costa Rica, and Honduras, before returning to the United States in April 1985 for a period of routine maintenance.

In August 1985, *Iowa* joined 160 other ships for Exercise Ocean Safari, a NATO naval exercise aimed at testing NATO's ability to control sea lanes and maintain free passage of shipping. Owing to bad weather, *Iowa* and the other ships were forced to ride out rough seas, but *Iowa* made use of the time to practice hiding herself from enemy forces. While serving with the exercise force, *Iowa* crossed the Arctic Circle.

In October, she took part in Baltic operations. After these operations, during which she visited LeHavre, France, Kiel, Germany, Copenhagen, Denmark, and Oslo. Norway where the King of Norway was entertained at lunch, she returned to the United States.

In December 1985, Cherneskey left the *Iowa* to assume the position of Director of Navy Programs in the Office of Legislative Affairs, Office of the Secretary of the Navy in Washington DC, remaining until May 1988. On July 6, 1988, Cherneskey relieved Captain James Carney to take command of the *Missouri*.

The remainder of the year would be spent conducting various inspections and readiness exercises out of Long Beach. After a dry dock maintenance period between February and April 1989, the *Missouri* was ordered to prepare for deployment, and departed California for the western Pacific on September 18.

After a voyage north to the Aleutian Islands in Alaska, she sailed for exercises in Japanese and Korean waters, visiting the port of Pusan October 21-25 before returning home on November 9. The *Missouri* then conducted a short cruise to Mazatlan, Mexico, in early December.

Missouri's next major operation took place on March 27, 1990, when she steamed to Hawaii to take part in Rim Pac'90, remaining in Hawaiian waters until returning home to Long Beach on May 23. On June 13, 1990, Cherneskey turned over command to Captain Albert Kaiss, and retired shortly thereafter, on September 1, 1990. His awards included the Legion of Merit with Gold Star, the Meritorious Service Medal with Gold Star, the Navy Commendation Medal with Gold Star and the Navy Achievement Medal with Gold Star.

After retiring, Cherneskey was the General Manager of the Los Angeles Shipyard Corporation from 1990 to 1992, Executive Director of the California Manufacturing Technology Center from 1992 to 1994 and from February 1994, Executive Director of Operations at the Cedars Sinai Comprehensive Cancer Center and later Chief Operating Officer of Salick Health Care in Los Angeles.

188

CAPTAIN JOHN J. CHERNESKEY

Cherneskey married Patricia Ann Wolf on October 7, 1967, and the couple had a daughter, Karen, and a son, John David, but the marriage didn't last, and he later married Melinda Brown. He died on December 13, 2001 at age 57, at his home in San Pedro, California, after losing his battle with kidney cancer. He was buried with full military honors at Arlington National Cemetery on Friday, January 4, 2002 in Section 66, Site 6529.

U.S.S. Missouri

Captain Albert Lee Kaiss
(Part Two)

It must have been a disappointment when Captain Albert Kaiss was forced to give up the helm of the Missouri, but it didn't end his naval career. He took assignment as the Mission Task Element Commander for the hospital ship USNS *Mercy* (T-AH-19). Built as a San Clemente-class oil tanker, SS *Worth* in 1976, she was renamed *Mercy* and converted to a hospital ship in July 1984.

The primary mission of the USNS *Mercy* is to provide rapid, flexible, and mobile acute medical and surgical services to support Marine Corps Air/Ground Task Forces deployed ashore, Army and Air Force units deployed ashore, and naval amphibious task forces and battle forces afloat.

Secondarily, she provides mobile surgical hospital service for use by appropriate US Government agencies in disaster and humanitarian relief, and limited humanitarian care incident to these missions and to peacetime military operations.

U.S.S. MISSOURI

On February 27, 1987, *Mercy* began a training mission while sailing to the Philippines and the South Pacific on a humanitarian cruise. The staff included U.S. Navy, Indian Navy, U.S. Army, and U.S. Air Force active duty and reserve personnel; United States Public Health Service; medical providers from the Armed Forces of the Philippines; and MSC civilian mariners.

Over 62,000 outpatients and almost 1,000 inpatients were treated at seven Philippine and South Pacific ports. *Mercy* returned to Oakland, California, in July 1987.

Following that, Kaiss served as Asst. Chief of Staff for Warfare and Tactics on the staff of Commander Naval Surface Force, until he was cleared to return to full duty in 1990. Kaiss's first tour as commanding officer of the *Missouri* had been cut short because of a medical problem, but unexpected events put him in the right place at the right time.

In June 1990, the *Missouri*'s commanding officer, Captain John Cherneskey decided to retire, and there was no planned relief in the pipeline. With Kaiss determined to be "fit for full duty" and fully qualified to command, the problem of a relief was resolved, and Kaiss returned to the "Mighty Mo" taking command for a second time on June 13, 1990.

In Response to Saddam Hussein's Iraqi Army invading Kuwait on August 2, 1990, the United States initiated Operation *Desert Shield*, a 35- nation coalition formed to oppose Iraq, the largest military alliance since World War II, and the *Missouri*'s crew began conducting security drills, installed more point defense weapons and began preparations for a Persian Gulf deployment, including familiarization with a newly embarked remotely piloted vehicle (RPV) drone.

Missouri got underway on November 13 and conducted intensive training in between stops at Pearl Harbor, Subic Bay and a liberty port visit to Pattaya Beach, Thailand, before transiting the Strait of Hormuz on January 3, 1991.

Her first mission upon arriving in the Persian Gulf was the disarming of a mine by her Explosive Ordnance Disposal (EOD) team on January 9, 1991. She then spent the period between January 8-15 underway in the Persian Gulf conducting a variety of operations.

CAPTAIN ALBERT LEE KAISS (PART TWO)

During operations leading up to Operation Desert Storm, Missouri prepared to launch *Tomahawk* missiles and provide on-call naval gunfire support. She fired her first *Tomahawk* missile at Iraqi targets at 1:40 am on January 17, aimed at Baghdad, followed by 13 additional missiles the next day. Over the next five days, she fired a total of 28 missiles.

On January 29, Iraqi forces captured the coastal town of Khafji in Saudi Arabia. Missouri steamed there to make certain that reinforcements could not reach the Iraqi forces.

On the night of February 3, *Missouri* bombarded Iraqi beach defenses in occupied Kuwait, firing her main battery in anger for the first time since the Korean War. She targeted concrete command-and-control bunkers as well as Iraqi artillery positions. Over the next three days, between February 5 and 7, she fired another 112 16-inch rounds until relieved by sister ship *Wisconsin* (BB 64).

On February 11-12, *Missouri* fired 60 rounds of 16-inch rounds during fire-support missions off Khafji. This time, her targets were infantry battalions, a mechanized unit, an artillery battery, and a command bunker. Afterwards, she headed north to near Faylaka Island, then under Iraqi control.

After having minesweepers clear a mine-free lane six miles long and one thousand yards wide through Iraqi defenses, *Missouri* fired 133 rounds during four shore bombardment missions as part of the amphibious landing feint against the Kuwaiti shore line on the morning of February 23.

193

U.S.S. MISSOURI

The heavy barrage gained the attention of the Iraqis, and they fired an HY-2 *Silkworm* missile at the battleship. The cruise missile was shot down by two GWS-30 *Sea Dart* missiles launched from the British frigate HMS *Gloucester.* It was the first time an anti-air missile had successfully engaged and destroyed an enemy missile during combat at sea. *Missouri* turned her 16-inch guns toward the Silkworm battery and destroyed her target.

On February 25, with combat operations moving inland past the range of the battleship's guns, *Missouri* performed patrol and armistice enforcement operations in the northern Persian Gulf. The land war by the Coalition forces proved successful and the Gulf War ended in a Coalition victory on February 28, 1991 and Missouri sailed for home on March 21.

In total, she fired Following stops at Fremantle and Hobart, Australia, the warship visited Pearl Harbor before arriving home at Long Beach on May 13, having been deployed for six months to the day.

Missouri spent the remainder of the year conducting training and other local operations, including being ordered to Hawaii for the December 7, 1991 "voyage of remembrance" to mark the 50th anniversary of the Pearl Harbor attack in 1941.

President Bush specifically desired the "Mighty Mo" to be present there as a symbol of the end of World War II and to host the official party during the event. During the ceremony, *Missouri* hosted President George H. W. Bush, himself a former naval aviator and WW II veteran. It was the first time a president had been aboard the warship since Harry Truman boarded her in September 1947. Being selected for this role was a moment of great pride for the crew.

The early morning ceremony at the USS *Arizona* memorial opened with President Bush reflecting on the courage and spirit of the American people on that day 50 years earlier. The ceremony concluded with the President and First Lady each placing a lei on the waters above the resting place of the sailors lost in the USS *Arizona* (BB-39).

After the ceremony, the President and his official party arrived on board the *Missouri.* At the request of the President, Captain Kaiss was the senior officer present, which helped focus the visitors on the fabled battleship and her superb crew. Security was tight, but President Bush interacted with the crew, and he addressed the nation from the surrender deck and then toured select areas of the ship.

Departure from Pearl Harbor was bittersweet with the knowledge that completion of the voyage would mark the end of the *Missouri*'s days at sea. For Captain Kaiss, it would be the last time both he and the *Missouri* were at sea as part of the active fleet. Retirement was the next step for the legendary ship and her commanding officer.

The collapse of the Soviet Union in the early 1990s and the absence of a perceived threat to the United States had resulted in drastic cuts to the defense budget, and the high cost of maintaining and operating battleships as part of the Navy's active fleet came to be perceived as extravagant and wasteful resulting in plans to decommission her. After returning to Long Beach on December 20, 1991, Kaiss and the crew began the long process of deactivating her. Missouri was decommissioned in a ceremony held on March 31, 1992.

That morning, 7,000 people gathered on the pier at the Long Beach Naval Station to say farewell to the Mighty Mo. Crew members who had been detached after the return from Pearl Harbor paid their own way back just to stand as part of the crew during the ceremony.

The Marine detachment that had so proudly served as part of the crew returned to carry the colors one last time. Hundreds of Missouri veterans from three wars returned for the final goodbye. The day was full of fond memories, pride, and sadness.

U.S.S. MISSOURI

Captain Albert L. Kaiss, wrote in the ship's final Plan of the Day:

"Our final day has arrived. Today the final chapter in battleship Missouri's history will be written. It's often said that the crew makes the command. There is no truer statement ... for it's the crew of this great ship that made this a great command. You are a special breed of sailors and Marines and I am proud to have served with each and every one of you. To you who have made the painful journey of putting this great lady to sleep, I thank you. For you have had the toughest job. To put away a ship that has become as much a part of you as you are to her is a sad ending to a great tour. But take solace in this—you have lived up to the history of the ship and those who sailed her before us. We took her to war, performed magnificently and added another chapter in her history, standing side by side our forerunners in true naval tradition. God bless you all."

The guest speaker at the decommissioning ceremony was Missouri Congressman Ike Skelton, who always had been a supporter of the Missouri and had been present at her recommissioning. His remarks highlighted her war record and the incredible performance of her crew throughout the years.

Kaiss then turned and addressed the executive officer, Captain Ken Jordon, *"XO, haul down the commissioning pennant and the colors. Upon completion, march off the crew."* Sailors lowered the colors for the last time and Kaiss positioned himself so he could see every crew member as they departed. He would say later that he wanted to remember every face.

Single file, they streamed off in reverse order of seniority with seamen, then petty officers, and finally the officers. The march-off completed, Kaiss turned to Lieutenant Commander Wes Carrie, the officer of the deck, and said, *"Secure the quarterdeck watch."* Carrie signed the deck log, then he, the petty officer of the watch, and the messenger departed the ship. Only one person remained on board.

Kaiss, eyes moist, the commissioning pennant held firmly in his left hand, took one final look around the main deck and then proceeded down the gangway. As he stepped onto the pier, he became the last active-duty battleship sailor.

CAPTAIN ALBERT LEE KAISS (PART TWO)

Captain Kaiss retired two days later, on April 2, 1992 after a thirty-year career that included combat action in Vietnam and in the Gulf War for which he was awarded a Legion of Merit and Bronze Star Medal with combat "V".

Following his retirement, Kaiss transitioned into civilian employment, working for eight years with Scientific Atlanta, and then serving with several companies, mentoring and training Naval Officers in ship-handling and ship safety before retiring again in 2013 and returning to Hagerstown, Md.

Kaiss was married to Veronica Resch with whom he had two children, a daughter Julie Veronica and a son, Andrew Lee. Albert Lee Kaiss passed away peacefully in his home on July 25, 2018 of natural causes. Services were held on Tuesday, July 31st at Saint Ann Catholic Church in Hagerstown, and he was buried at Mountain View Cemetery in Sharpsburg, Maryland with Military Honors. As his daughter remembered him in her eulogy *"He loved to teach...he loved to solve problems."*

U.S.S. MISSOURI

Battleship Missouri Museum & Memorial

Following her decommissioning on March 31,1992, the USS *Missouri* was placed in the inactive reserve fleet at Puget Sound Naval Shipyard, Bremerton, Washington. She remained part of the reserve fleet until January 12, 1995 when she was stricken from the Naval Vessel Register.

The ship remained at Bremerton, but the Missouri was **not** open to tourists as she had been from 1957 to 1984. Citizen groups advocated keeping her in Bremerton and re-opening her as a tourist site, but the U.S. Navy had plans to pair a symbol of the end of World War II with one representing its beginning at Pearl Harbor. Donated as a museum and memorial ship on May 4, 1998, *Missouri* was later transferred to Pearl Harbor where the old battleship rests near the *Arizona* (BB-39) Memorial and is open for tours by the public.

On May 4. 1998, Secretary of the Navy John H. Dalton signed the donation contract that transferred her ownership from the US Navy to the nonprofit USS Missouri Memorial Association (MMA) of Honolulu, Hawaii.

U.S.S. Missouri

She was towed from Bremerton on May 23 to Astoria, Oregon, where she sat in fresh water at the mouth of the Columbia River in order to kill and drop the saltwater barnacles and sea grasses that had grown on her hull while docked at Bremerton.

Afterwards, she was towed across the eastern Pacific, and docked at Ford Island, Pearl Harbor on June 22, 1998, just 500 yds from the *Arizona* Memorial. Less than a year later, on January 29, 1999, *Missouri* was opened as a museum operated by the MMA.

Originally, the decision to move *Missouri* to Pearl Harbor was met with some resistance from the National Park Service which expressed concerns that the battleship, whose name has become synonymous with the end of World War II, would overshadow the battleship USS *Arizona*, whose dramatic explosion and subsequent sinking on December 7, 1941, has become synonymous with the attack on Pearl Harbor.

To help prevent this impression, *Missouri* was positioned well back from and facing the Arizona Memorial. The decision to have *Missouri*'s bow face the Arizona Memorial was intended to convey the idea that the *Missouri* watches over the remains of *Arizona* so that those interred within *Arizona*'s hull may rest in peace.

On January 29, 1999, after six months of repair and restoration, *Missouri* was opened as a museum operated by the USS

Missouri Memorial Association, Inc. (MMA) which is a non-profit 501(c)3 corporation established in the State of Hawaii in 1994.

The two key purposes of the Association were initially to *"relocate the USS Missouri (BB-63) to Hawaii to establish, operate and maintain a national memorial commemorating the end of hostilities in World War II to serve as a lasting tribute to the United States Navy's role in forging world peace through strength"* and to *"operate exclusively for charitable, scientific, literary, or educational purposes, within the meaning of Section 501 (c)3 of the Internal Revenue Code of 1986."*

The Association receives no funding from either the U.S. Navy or any other governmental agency for the operations or ongoing maintenance of the ship. The mission of the Association is dedicated to the preservation of the Battleship Missouri and sharing her story and place in history.

The *Missouri* was listed on the National Register of Historic Places on May 14, 1971 for hosting the signing of the instrument of Japanese surrender that ended World War II. She is not eligible for designation as a National Historic Landmark because she was extensively modernized in the years following the surrender.

Visitors to the museum can take a 35-minute Guided Tour or explore the ship on their own. Areas of interest include the gun mounts, the "Surrender Deck" and more than 100 stops above and below decks, including the engine rooms, gun turret #1, the galley, crew's quarters, damage control central station, Broadway, fire room #4 and the aft battery plot room. Tour guides and staff are available to answer questions or give directions and informational signs are located throughout the ship.

The USS *Missouri* continues to live in the popular culture. *Missouri* was central to the plot of the film *Under Siege*, although many scenes were shot aboard the battleship USS *Alabama*. The *Missouri* was also prominently featured in another movie, *Battleship*. As *Missouri* has not moved under her own power since 1992, shots of the ship at sea were obtained with the help of three tugboats.

The music video for Cher's "If I Could Turn Back Time" was also filmed aboard *Missouri*. The Navy had granted permission to shoot the video there but was less than pleased with the sexual nature of her performance.

But it must be remembered that before she was a museum, *Missouri* was a warship that served in three wars and received three battle stars for her service in World War II, five for her service during the Korean War, and three for her service during the Gulf War and also received numerous other awards for her service in World War II, Korea, and the Persian Gulf.

In her years of service, Missouri gave truth to the words of President Theodore Roosevelt: *"A good Navy is not a provocation to war. It is the surest guaranty of peace."*

Made in the USA
Middletown, DE
16 December 2022

18938459R00119